To the partnership
that brought this book about

Ralph L. Rosnow is the Thaddeus Bolton Professor of Psychology at Temple University and has also taught at Boston University and Harvard University. He has written numerous books and journal articles.

Mimi Rosnow took her undergraduate degree in English at Wheaton College in Norton, Massachusetts. She has done freelance editorial consulting and for a number of years was an editorial assistant at a national magazine.

Contents

808.066
ROS

TH EDITION

Writing Papers in Psychology

A STUDENT GUIDE

Ralph L. Rosnow
Temple University

Mimi Rosnow

Wadsworth
Thomson Learning

Australia • Canada • Mexico • Singapore • Spain • United Kingdom • United States

Psychology Publisher: Vicki Knight
Marketing Manager: Marc Linsenman
Project Editor: Matt Stevens
Print Buyer: Mary Noel
Permissions Editor: Joohee Lee
Production Service: Forbes Mill Press

Text Designer: Robin Gold
Copy Editor: Margaret Ritchie
Cover Designer: Liz Harasymczuk
Compositor: Wolf Creek Press
Printer/Binder: Webcom, Ltd.

Printed in Canada

1 2 3 4 5 6 03 02 01 00

ISBN 0-534-52975-5

For more information, contact
Wadsworth/Thomson Learning
10 Davis Drive
Belmont, CA 94002-3098
USA
www.wadsworth.com

International Headquarters
Thomson Learning
International Division
290 Harbor Drive, 2nd Floor
Stamford, CT 06902-7477
USA

UK/Europe/Middle East
Thomson Learning
Berkshire House
168-173 High Holborn
London WC1V 7AA
United Kingdom

Asia
Thomson Learning
60 Albert Street, #15-01
Albert Complex
Singapore 189969

Canada
Nelson/Thomson Learning
1120 Birchmount Road
Toronto, Ontario M1K 5G4
Canada

Exhibits

Preface

Writing Papers in Psychology began as a handout designed to help students write research reports back in the days when word processors were called typewriters. Typewriters are artifacts of an earlier generation, and in updating this fifth edition, we emphasize technological advances within the grasp of this generation of students. Guided by the following flowchart, students can refer to specific chapters and selections as needed:

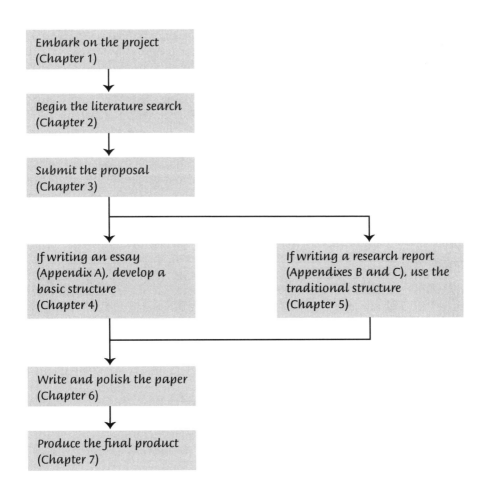

Embark on the project
(Chapter 1)

Begin the literature search
(Chapter 2)

Submit the proposal
(Chapter 3)

If writing an essay
(Appendix A), develop a
basic structure
(Chapter 4)

If writing a research report
(Appendixes B and C), use the
traditional structure
(Chapter 5)

Write and polish the paper
(Chapter 6)

Produce the final product
(Chapter 7)

Recommended Style

Except for two small departures, the recommended style is the one spelled out in the *Publication Manual of the American Psychological Association* (1994, 4th edition), while statistical results reported in the two research papers (in Appendixes B and C) conform to the guidelines suggested by the APA's Task Force on Statistical Inference (*American Psychologist*, 1999, Vol. 54, pp. 594–604). One departure from the APA publication manual is that an appendix is recommended at the end of the research report for the student's raw data calculations and any coding sheets or research materials created by the student. The second departure is the recommended cover page of the paper, which contains information of relevance to the course and the instructor. In all other respects, the format is identical to that recommended in the APA publication manual.

In fact, the APA is actually rather flexible in many of its stylistic requirements, at least as indicated by various responses to questions appearing on the APA Publication Manual Web site (http://www.apa.org/journals/faq.html). For example, a student asked whether the title shown on the title page of a manuscript belongs in the middle of the page or closer to the top of the page, since the student had noticed that "colleagues' versions of the Publication Manual show a different graphic for the title page of a manuscript." The APA's response was that either one was correct. Another person asked why underlining rather than italics was required, because a word processor makes it just as easy to italicize as underline. The APA's answer was that underlining signals to the typesetter to use italics, but that if a manuscript for publication is in final form, it is quite acceptable to use the italicizing function to mimic what would be typeset in italics and to improve the appearance of the manuscript. In this book we generally recommend that students underline statistical symbols and algebraic variables. However, the APA policy is not to return a manuscript in which italics are used, because once the paper is accepted for publication the APA copyeditor inserts an underline anyway.

We also recommend using a regular paragraph-type indent when creating references, as specified in the APA publication manual. Interestingly, however, the APA's Web site response to a question about this practice was "If you are preparing a manuscript in final form, meaning that the manuscript will not later be typeset and published, you may prefer to format references with a hanging indent to enhance readability." In other words, there is leeway at APA in what is permissible. In the spirit of APA's commonsense flexibility, we encourage flexibility on the part of instructors. The rule of thumb that has guided us is utility. Thus, *Writing Papers* is designed to make the process of conceptualizing, writing, and producing a paper meaningful and palatable to students in a way they will also find useful in the future.

New to this edition is Chapter Two, which in previous editions was simply called "Using the Library" and in this edition has a broader emphasis using new and traditional resources to do a literature search. There is also further advice on ethical guidelines, including a discussion of plagiarism and how to avoid it. In fact, all the chapters and sample papers have been reworked to reflect the style recommended by the APA publication manual (4th edition) and the assumption that students are using a word-processing program (such as Microsoft Word). Instructors have told us they use *Writing Papers* to usher graduate students into the APA style, and we have added a few ideas with that objective in mind. If students are preparing papers to be submitted for publication, we again recommend they read the most recent edition of R. J. Sternberg's *Psychologist's Companion* (Cambridge University Press)—an engaging introduction to all aspects of professional writing by a noted psychologist who has been successful in all of them. Whether the student is writing for a course or a journal, the classic reference for style is W. Strunk, Jr., and E. B. White's *Elements of Style* (Prentice-Hall)—a gem of a book that belongs on every writer's desk.

Acknowledgments

We thank three outstanding teachers—Drs. Anne Skleder (Alvernia College), Bruce Rind (Temple University), and Peter Crabb (Penn State University, Abington-Ogontz)—for preparing drafts of the sample papers at the end of this book. We thank MaryLu Rosenthal for advising us through all five editions about the methods and means available for a literature search in a modern college library, and we thank Richard Lezenby of Temple University's Paley Library for his assistance. We thank Eric Foster, for allowing us to look over his shoulder in Chapter Two, and Dr. Ram Aditya (Louisiana Tech University), for permitting us to describe the literature review he did when he was a graduate student working on his master's thesis. We thank the following consultants, whose suggestions have improved one or more editions of our book: Drs. John B. Best (Eastern Illinois University), David E. Campbell (Humboldt State University), Scott D. Churchill (University of Dallas), Nicholas DiFonzo (Rochester Institute of Technology), Nancy Eldred (San Jose State University), Robert Gallen (Georgetown College), David Goldstein (Duke University), John Hall (Texas Wesleyan University), James W. Kalat (North Carolina State University), Allan J. Kimmel (École Supérieure de Commerce de Paris), Arlene Lundquist (Mount Union College), Joann Montepare (Tufts University), Quentin Newhouse, Jr. (Bowie State University), Arthur Nonneman (Asbury College), Edgar O'Neal (Tulane University), Wendy Palmquist (Plymouth State College), Rick Pollack (Merrimack College), Maureen Powers (Vanderbilt University), Jackson Rainer (Gardner-Webb University), Robert Rosenthal (University of California at Riverside), Gordon W. Russell (University of Lethbridge), Steven Schandler (Chapman College), Helen Shoemaker (California State University at Hayward), John Sparrow (State University of New York at Geneseo), Jutta Street (Barton College), David Strohmetz (Monmouth University), and Stephen A. Truhon (Winston-Salem State University). We are grateful to Vicki Knight for her interest and enthusiasm for this project, and to Ken King and James Brace-Thompson for their support of the previous editions of this book. Once again, we thank Margaret Ritchie for her skillful editing.

We do not always specify the publication dates for reference books in our own narrative but instead advise students to seek the latest edition available and thus avoid consulting outdated material. In addition to the APA *Publication Manual*, we also found the following books helpful in reminding us of technical points we might have forgotten to mention: R. Barrass, *Scientists Must Write* (Wiley, 1978); R. W. Bly and G. Blake, *Technical Writing: Structure, Standard, and Style* (McGraw-Hill, 1982); V. Dumond, *Elements of Nonsexist Usage: A Guide to Inclusive Spoken and Written English* (Prentice Hall, 1990); B. L. Ellis, *How to Write Themes and Term Papers* (Barron's, 1989); D. E. Fear, *Technical Writing* (Random House, 1973); H. R. Fowler, *The Little, Brown Handbook* (Little, Brown, 1983); J. Gibaldi and W. S. Achtert, *MLA Handbook for Writers of Research Papers* (Modern Language Association, 1988); K. W. Houp and T. E. Pearsall, *Reporting Technical Information* (Macmillan, 1984); C. Hult and J. Harris, *A Writer's Introduction to Word Processing* (Wadsworth, 1987); S. Kaye, *Writing Under Pressure: The Quick Writing Process* (Oxford University Press, 1989); M. H. Markel, *Technical Writing: Situations and Strategies* (St. Martin's Press, 1984); M. McCormick, *The New York Times Guide to Reference Materials* (Dorset, 1985); D. J. D. Mulkerne and D. J. D. Mulkerne, Jr., *The Term Paper* (Anchor/Doubleday, 1983); L. A. Olsen and T. N. Huchin, *Principles of Communication for Science and Technology* (McGraw-Hill, 1957); J. G. Reed and P. M. Baxter, *Library Use: A Handbook for Psychology* (American Psychological Association, 1992); B. Spatt, *Writing from Sources* (St. Martin's Press, 1987); K. L. Turabian, *A Manual for Writers of Term Papers, Theses and Dissertations* (University of Chicago Press, 1955); and J. E. Warriner, *Handbook of English* (Harcourt, Brace, 1951).

Finally, we thank the many users of this manual. Your comments and suggestions have helped us to improve each new edition. We again invite instructors and students to send us comments and suggestions for further improvements.

Ralph L. Rosnow
Mimi Rosnow

Chapter One

GETTING STARTED

Writing papers to fulfill course requirements means knowing what is expected of you and then formulating a plan to accomplish your goal on schedule. This chapter includes some simple dos and don'ts to help you avoid pitfalls and to ensure that the assignment will be completed on time and that it will represent your best work.

Where to Begin

There was once an intriguing character named Joe Gould, who, after graduating from Harvard in 1911 and trying his hand at a number of failed endeavors, moved to New York and began to hang around Greenwich Village coffee shops. He told people that he had mastered the language of seagulls, and in fact he did an uncanny imitation of one. He was best known, however, for an ambitious project he claimed to be compiling, called the "Oral History of Our Times." He boasted of having accumulated a stack of notebooks that stood seven feet tall, and he carried brown paper bags with him that, he said, contained research notes.

Joe Gould died in a psychiatric hospital while doing his seagull imitation. Some years later, in a *New Yorker* profile by Joseph Mitchell and then in a book by Mitchell entitled *Joe Gould's Secret* (Modern Library, 1996), it was revealed that Joe Gould never started his "Oral History," his notebooks were a myth, and his brown bags merely contained other bags and yellowed newspaper clippings. For students with required writing assignments, Joe Gould is a metaphor for the most challenging aspect of any project: how to get started.

To begin your project, you need some clear objectives. Here is a checklist of questions to focus your approach:

◆ What is the purpose of the required assignment?
◆ Do I choose the theme or topic, or will it be assigned by the instructor?
◆ How long should the paper be?

- Will interim papers (for example, a proposal and progress reports) be required, and when are they due?
- When is the final report due, and how does this date mesh with my other requirements (for example, exams and other papers)?

You can talk with other students about their impressions, but the person who knows *exactly* what is expected of you is the instructor. Before you turn on a word processor or sharpen any pencils, articulate what you understand the assignment to be and ask the instructor if your understanding is accurate. One instructor wrote to us that many of his students were reluctant to take this initial step, even though they hadn't a clue about a topic for a paper. But those who did come in, even without an idea for a topic, benefited from a meeting and, in most cases, went away at least with the beginning of a direction for their papers.

Focusing on Your Objective

Once you have a topic, thinking through the assignment will sharpen the intellectual process. To help you focus on your particular objective, it is well to understand the differences between the essay and the research report and the different varieties of each of these forms. We suggest you pause at this point and read the sample papers in the three appendixes at the end of this book, as we will be referring to them repeatedly. If you are writing an undergraduate thesis or a master's thesis, your paper will probably contain features of *both* essays and research reports. Let us start with the general differences between the essay and the research report (see Exhibit 1), so you can concentrate your efforts on whichever project you have been assigned.

One distinction highlighted in Exhibit 1 is that a literature search usually forms the core of the essay, whereas data form the core of the research report. The literature search for the research report typically involves a few key studies that serve as a theoretical starting point, so you can expect to spend more time in the library if you are writing an essay. Of course, you still must spend time in the library if you are writing a research report, because you will need to look up

EXHIBIT 1   Differences between essays and research reports

Essay	Research Report
1. Is based on literature search; no hard data of your own to interpret	1. Is based on data that you have collected; literature search involving only a few key studies
2. Is structured by you to fit your particular topic	2. Is structured to follow a traditional form
3. Puts ideas into the context of a particular thesis	3. Reports your own research findings to others

background information. If you are writing an undergraduate thesis or a master's thesis, you will be expected to do a thorough search of the relevant literature. We will show how this is done in the next chapter.

A second distinction is that the composition of the essay, although somewhat formal, is more flexible than that of the research report, which has a much more standardized structure. The structure of an essay needs to be flexible because there are different types of essays that represent quite different objectives. Instructors expect the structure of the research report to conform to a general tradition that has evolved over many years. As a consequence, research reports typically include an abstract (that is, a brief summary), an introduction, a method section, a results section, a discussion of the results, and a list of the references cited.

The final distinction noted in Exhibit 1 is that the essay puts issues and ideas into the context of a particular theme or thesis, whereas the objective of the research report is to describe your empirical investigation to others. The theme in a research report usually involves testable hypotheses. What you found in your research must be put into the context of these hypotheses, but not by the same approach used when writing an essay. We will have more to say about this last point later.

Three Types of Essays

If this were a course in the English department, you would be taught about three types of essays: the expository, the argumentative, and the case study. Each has its own objective. In psychology courses, however, student essays are often expected to have some characteristics of more than just one type. For example, Anne Skleder's sample paper in Appendix A (beginning on page 95) has at least a flavor of all three types, although it is primarily an expository essay.

First, the objective of an *expository essay* is to inform the reader on a specific subject or theme—in Anne's case, two views of intelligence. The word *expository* means "expounding," "setting forth," or "explaining." Expository essays call for accessibility in writing—like the articles that are in the science section of the *New York Times* each Tuesday, but in more detail and with full citations. Anne does not begin by writing, "I am going to explain two views of intelligence." That is, in fact, her aim (implicit in the title of her paper), but her opening paragraph shows elegance and artistry and thus draws the reader into the exposition. Other examples of expository essays might be "Basic Differences Between Operant and Classical Conditioning" and "The Role of the Teacher's Expectations in Students' Academic Performance." Each title promises to inform the reader about some topic.

Second, the objective of persuading the reader to accept a particular point of view calls for an *argumentative essay*. In Anne's paper, there is an implicit argument for what she terms the "multiplex approach." Another example of this type of essay might be one that argued the cost-effectiveness of behavior therapy versus a more time-consuming psychotherapeutic approach. In psychology courses, argumentative essays usually attempt either to advance or to challenge the applicability of some theoretical idea to a realm beyond the one it was intended for. Such essays ask readers either to form a new view or to change their minds about a particular theoretical idea. If you are writing a primarily argumentative essay, be sure to express all viewpoints fairly, and not just in a "take it or leave it" fashion. Show that you recognize gray areas as you develop your position, and present documentation to support it. If you are arguing against a particular viewpoint, you can collect specific quotations to illustrate that you have represented it accurately. Otherwise, you might be accused of making a "straw man argument," which means that you represented the other side in a false, unfair, or misleading way to buttress your personal view. Before you begin to write, it is usually a good idea to argue your point of view with someone who is a good listener and promises to be critical. Jot down questions and counterarguments while they are fresh in your mind so that you can deal with them in your paper.

Third, the purpose of the *descriptive essay* is to define (or describe) its topics. Describing (defining) the topic is a part of virtually every essay and research report, although in the descriptive essay it is the sole (or at least the primary) aim. Generally speaking, descriptive essays are frequently (but not always) shorter than expository or argumentative essays, and it is not often that a purely descriptive essay is required as a term paper. Articles in encyclopedias resemble descriptive essays. In areas of clinical psychology, you will find various combinations of descriptive and expository forms in case study reports (which are also descriptive research reports). If you are interested in reading classic examples, start with Sigmund Freud's essays, such as his case study of the "Wolf-Man," a Russian aristocrat who as a youth developed a wolf phobia and as an adult was psychoanalyzed by Freud (*The Wolf-Man and Sigmund Freud,* edited by M. Gardiner, Penguin Books, 1973).

Incidentally, creative ability is valued in science just as it is in English courses. But when explaining or describing in science, you want to be accurate and avoid flights of fancy. An effective essay in psychology is also not vague but incorporates specific examples and exact quotations to support ideas.

Three Types of Research Reports

Researchers make fine distinctions among the various kinds of research approaches, such as the laboratory experiment, the field experiment, the sample survey approach, the intensive case study, and the archival study. The sample paper by Bruce in Appendix B (a field experiment) and the paper by Peter in Appendix C (an archival study) illustrate two such approaches, each reporting actual data. Over and above these fine differences is another distinction among three broad types of research: the descriptive, the relational, and the experimental. Each of these has its own objective, reflected in the research report, although the report may also contain a flavor of more than one type.

First, the purpose of the *descriptive research report* (like that of the descriptive essay) is to map out its subject. In Appendix C, Peter's report describes the content of pictorial representations of gender and work in children's books. The focus of the report is descriptive, but mapping out the relation between gender and type of work activity implies a kind of relational flavor. Another illustration of a descriptive study would be a report of observations of freshman students thrown together for the first time as roommates in a dormitory. As another example, an education student or a psychology student specializing in child psychology might be interested in studying children's failure in school and might begin by spending a good deal of time observing the classroom behavior of children who were doing poorly. Careful mapping out of the behavior of failing pupils might lead to theoretical ideas about how to revise our concepts of classroom failure, to suggestions of factors that may have contributed to the development of failure, and perhaps to hypotheses for relational and experimental research concerning the remediation of failure.

The careful description of behavior is usually a necessary first step in the development of a program of research. Sooner or later, however, someone will want to know *how* what happens behaviorally is related to other variables. The how is the subject of the *relational research report,* which examines how events are related or how behavior is correlated with another variable. An example might be the report of an observational study of how first-year college students have behaved differently toward one another over time; the factor of time would be one variable, and the students' behavior would be the correlated variable. In our other continuing example, the education or psychology student who is interested in failure in school might note for each pupil (a) whether the child was learning and (b) the degree to which the teacher had been exposing the child to the material to be learned. The finished report would examine the relationship between (b) and (a), that is, the amount of the pupils' exposure to the material to be learned and the amount of such material that they did in fact learn.

Thus, we can say that descriptive reports tell *how things are,* whereas relational reports tell *how things are in relation to other things.* The purpose of the third type, the *experimental research report,* is to tell *how things get to be the way they are.* Bruce's report (in Appendix B) of a field experiment on the effect of being offered an after-meal candy on tipping behavior illustrates this objective. Another experimental example would be if you were interested in doing laboratory research with animals; you might report on how social behavior in rats is affected by manipulation of the animals' reinforcement schedules. If Peter's descriptive study (Appendix C) whets your interest, you might develop an experiment (as he implies at the end of his paper) to examine how pictorial illustrations of work episodes affect children's expectations, attitudes, and behavior.

Scheduling Time

Once you have a clear sense of your objective, the next step is to set some deadlines so you do not end up like Joe Gould, who was so paralyzed by inertia that he accomplished nothing. In *The Shaping of a Behaviorist* (New York University Press, 1984), the celebrated psychologist B. F. Skinner recollected how he had sought to discipline himself by developing a very strict regimen when he entered Harvard University as a graduate student in 1928:

> I had done what was expected of me in high school and college but had seldom worked hard. Aware that I was far behind in a new field, I now set up a rigorous schedule and maintained it for almost two years. I would rise at six, study until breakfast, go to classes, laboratories, and libraries with no more than fifteen minutes unscheduled during the day, study until exactly nine o'clock at night and go to bed. (p. 5)

No one expects you to develop a schedule as stringent as Skinner's was when he was a student. However, once you know what is expected of you, you need to set specific deadlines that you feel you can meet. You know your own energy level and thought patterns, so play to your strengths. Are you a morning person? If so, block out some time to work on your writing early in the day. Do you function better at night? Then use the late hours of quiet to your advantage. Allow extra time for other pursuits by setting realistic dates by which you can reasonably expect to complete each major part of your assignment. Write the dates on your calendar; many students also find it useful to post the dates over their desks as daily reminders.

How do you know what tasks to schedule? If you look again at the three papers in Appendixes A, B, and C, you will infer that writing an essay calls for quite a different schedule from writing a research report. Writing an essay requires spending a lot of time in the library accumulating source materials, so you will need to leave ample time for that task. Here are some hints about what to schedule on your calendar:

Completion of proposal for essay
Completion of library work
Completion of first draft of essay
Completion of revised draft(s) of essay
Completion of final draft of essay

If you are writing a research report, set aside time for these major tasks:

Completion of proposal for research
Completion of ethics review
Completion of data collection
Completion of data analysis
Completion of first draft of research report
Completion of revised draft(s) of research report
Completion of final draft of research report

Note that both schedules of tasks allow time between the first and final drafts to distance yourself from your writing. Organizing, writing, and revising will take time. Library research does not always go smoothly; a book or a journal article you need might be unavailable. Data collection and analysis can also run into snags. Notice in Bruce's paper that, in the last sentence of his Results section, he mentions having consulted with the instructor about doing further data analyses; the instructor has advised him not to attempt them (because there will not be enough time for Bruce to complete them and still have time to write and polish his final draft). Other snags might be that the ethics review takes longer than you expected, or research subjects might not cooperate, or a computer you need might be down, or research material you need is hard to find. These schedules allow you time to cope with unforeseen problems like these and time to return to your writing assignment with a fresh perspective as you polish the first draft and check for errors in logic, flow, spelling, punctuation, and grammar. By scheduling your time in this way, you should not feel pressured by imaginary deadlines—or surprised as the real deadline approaches.

If you get started early, you will also have time to track down hard-to-find reports (called the *fugitive literature* in the next chapter) or to locate a test you need. If you want to use a specific instrument protected by copyright, you will need to give yourself time to get written permission from the publisher to use the test. Instruments that require advanced training to administer or interpret are usually unavailable to undergraduate students, but there are a great many psychological measures that *are* available to students. For example, if you were doing empirical research in social or personality psychology, two relevant books might be M. E. Shaw and J. M. Wright's *Scales for the Measurement of Attitudes* (McGraw-Hill, 1967) and J. P. Robinson, P. R. Shaver, and L. S. Wrightsman's *Measures of Personality and Social Psychological Attitudes* (Academic Press, 1991). Each book contains useful paper-and-pencil measures and provides information about the validity and reliability of each measure.

For a catalog of tests and measures that you can find in journal articles and reports, see the *Directory of Unpublished Experimental Mental Measures* (American Psychological Association, Vols. 1–6, 1995–1996). Volume 6, compiled by B. A. Goldman and D. F. Mitchell, lists nearly 1,700 psychological instruments that are available for use in a wide variety of research situations, including measures of educational, psychological, social, and vocational adjustment, and measures of aptitude, attitude, concept meaning, creativity, personality, problem solving, status, and so on. Exhibit 2 shows six measures from this volume, and enough information is given to help you track down any particular instrument.

Starting early may also give you time to tackle data analysis procedures that are not in the course textbook. For example, both Bruce (Appendix B) and Peter (Appendix C) looked outside their textbooks to find specialized methods for statistical analyses of their data. There will also be time to write to an author for follow-up articles if you think you need them. (Many students

EXHIBIT 2   Synopses of experimental mental measures

3678
Test Name: JOB CAREER KEY

Purpose: To provide a test of information about a wide variety of occupations.

Number of Items: 157

Format: A multiple-choice format is used

Reliability: Kuder-Richardson formulas ranged from .43 to .91. Test–retest (4 months) reliability (N = 19) was .62.

Author: Yanico, B. J., and Hardin, S. I.

Article: College students' self-estimated and actual knowledge of gender traditional and nontraditional occupation: A replication and extension.

Journal: *Journal of Vocational Behavior,* June 1986, 28(3), 229–240.

Related Research: Blank, J. R. (1978). Job-career key: A test of occupational information. *Vocational Guidance Quarterly, 27,* 6–17.

3723
Test Name: MEIER BURNOUT ASSESSMENT

Purpose: To measure college student burnout.

Number of Items: 27

Format Employs a true-false format.

Reliability: Cronbach's alpha was .83.

Validity: Correlations with other variables ranged from -.13 to .62 (N = 360).

Author: McCarthy, M. E., et al.

Article: Psychological sense of community and student burnout.

Journal: *Journal of College Student Development,* May 1990, 31(3), 211–216

Related Research: Meier, S. T., & Schmeck, R. R. (1985). The burned-out college student: A descriptive profile. *Journal of College Student Personnel, 25,* 63–69.

3705
Test Name: COMPUTER ANXIETY SCALE

Purpose: To measure the perception held by students of their anxiety in different situations related to computers.

Number of Items: 20

Format: Each item is rated on a 5-point scale ranging from *not at all* to *very much.* All items are presented.

Reliability: Test-retest (10 weeks) reliability was .77. Coefficient alpha was .97.

Author: Marcoulides, G. A.

Article: Measuring computer anxiety: The Computer Anxiety Scale.

Journal: *Educational and Psychological Measurement,* Autumn 1989, 49(3), 733–739.

Related Research: Endler, N., & Hunt, J. (1966). Sources of behavioral variance as measured by the S-R Inventory of Anxiousness. *Psychological Bulletin, 65,* 336–339.

3993
Test Name: DATING ANXIETY SURVEY

Purpose: To assess dating anxiety in males and females.

Number of Items: 23

Format: Responses are made on a 7-point Likert scale, 1 (*being least anxious*) to 7 (*being extreme anxiety*). Includes three subscales: passive, active, and dating.

Reliability: Coefficient alphas ranged from .87 to .93 (males) and from .90 to .92 (females).

Validity: Correlations with other variables ranged from −.38 to .65.

Author: Calvert, J. D., et al.

Article: Psychometric evaluations of the Dating Anxiety Survey: A self-report questionnaire for the assessment of dating anxiety in males and females.

Journal: *Journal of Psychopathology and Behavioral Assessment,* September 1987, 9(3), 341–350.

3710
Test Name: HASSLES SCALE

Purpose: To identify the personal severity of daily hassles as an index of student stress.

Number of items: 117

Format: Respondents indicate on a 3-point scale the severity of each relevant daily hassle. Provides two scores: frequency and intensity.

Reliability: Average test-retest reliabilities were .79 (frequency) and .48 (intensity).

Author: Elliott, T. R., and Gramling, S. E.

Article: Personal assertiveness and the effects of social support among college students.

Journal: *Journal of Counseling Psychology,* October 1990, 37(4), 427–436.

Related Research: Kanner, A., et al. (1981). Comparison of two modes of stress measurement: Daily hassles and uplifts versus major life events. *Journal of Behavioral Medicine, 4,* 1–39.

4431
Test Name: PROCRASTINATION INVENTORY

Purpose: To measure procrastination in work-study, household chores, and interpersonal responsibilities.

Number of Items: 54

Format: Five-point self-rating scales. Sample items presented.

Reliability: Alpha was .91.

Validity: Correlations with other variables ranged from .41 (self-control) to .62 (effective study time).

Author: Stoham-Salomon, V., et al.

Article: You're changed if you do and changed if you don't: Mechanisms underlying paradoxical interventions.

Journal: *Journal of Consulting and Clinical Psychology,* October, 1989, 57(5), 590–598.

Related Research: Sroloff, B. (1963). *An empirical research of procrastination as a state/trait phenomenon.* Unpublished Master's Thesis, Tel-Aviv University, Israel.

---

are surprised to learn that they can actually write to an author of a research study and ask about the author's most recent work.) Another word of advice: Instructors have heard all the excuses for a late or badly done paper, so do not expect much sympathy if you miss the final deadline. If you expect to ask the instructor for a letter of recommendation for graduate school or a job, you certainly do not want to create an impression of yourself as unreliable.

Choosing a Topic

The next step is to choose a suitable topic. The selection of a topic is an integral part of learning, because usually you are free to explore experiences, observations, and ideas to help you focus on specific questions or issues that will sustain your curiosity and interest as you work on your project. If you want to play detective, you may find prematurely abandoned ideas in research articles, such as when the researchers used statistical tests that were insensitive to the obtained effects. If you suspect this problem, you can look for clues using only a calculator and the raw ingredients in the published article. To learn more about how to do this kind of detecting, see R. L. Rosnow and R. Rosenthal's "Computing Contrasts, Effect Sizes, and Counternulls on Other People's Published Data: General Procedures for Research Consumers" (*Psychological Methods,* 1996, Vol. 1, pp. 331–340).

Ideas can also be thrust on us in unexpected ways—called *serendipity,* which is a lucky inspiration. The word comes from a fairy tale about "The Three Princes of Serendip" (an ancient name for Ceylon, now known as Sri Lanka), who were constantly making lucky discoveries. A book on this subject is *Serendipity: Accidental Discoveries in Science,* by R. M. Roberts (Wiley, 1989). A famous case of serendipity occurred in James Watson and Francis Crick's race (with Linus Pauling) to discover the structure of the DNA molecule and win the Nobel Prize. Watson made cardboard models, which he showed to a colleague, Jerry Donohue, a crystallographer who shared an office with Crick. Donohue's response was that the models contained mistakes, and Watson went home feeling discouraged. The next day, he was back in his office tinkering with another model when Donohue happened to walk in. Watson asked Donohue whether he had any objections to it, and when he answered no, Watson's morale soared, as he realized that he might now have the answer to the DNA riddle. In *The Double Helix* (Atheneum, 1968), Watson wrote that, had it not been for the lucky dividend of Donohue's sharing an office with Crick, Crick and Watson would not have won this race for the Nobel Prize.

In considering a suitable topic, beware of a few pitfalls; the following are dos and don'ts that might make your life easier as you start choosing a topic:

- ◆ Use the indexes and tables of contents of standard textbooks as well as your class notes for initial leads or ideas to explore more fully.
- ◆ Choose a topic that piques your curiosity.

- Make sure your topic can be covered in the available time and in the assigned number of pages.
- Don't be afraid to ask your instructor for suggestions.
- Don't choose a topic that you know other students have chosen; you will be competing with them for access to the library's source material.

Shaping the Topic

Choosing too broad or too narrow a topic will surely add difficulties and will also mean an unsatisfactory result. A proposed essay that is too broad—for example, "Freud's Life and Times"—would try to cover too much material within the limited framework of the assignment and the time available to complete it. A specific aspect of Freud's theoretical work would prove a more appropriately narrowed focus for treatment in an essay for a course requirement.

In narrowing the essay topic, do not limit your discussion just to facts that are already well known. There are two simple guidelines:

- Be sure that your topic is not so narrow that reference materials will be hard to find.
- Be guided by your instructor's advice because the instructor can help you avoid taking on an unwieldy topic.

If you approach instructors with several concrete ideas, you will usually find them glad to help tailor those ideas so that you, the topic, and the project format are compatible. Here are examples of how you might shape the working title of a proposed essay for a one-semester course on personality theories:

Unlimited Topic (Much Too Broad)
"Psychological Theories of Sigmund Freud"

Slightly Limited Topic
"Freud's Theory of Dreams"

Limited to 20-Page Paper
"Freud's Theory of Oedipal Conflict Applied to Mental Health"

Limited to 10-Page Paper
"Freud's Theory of Infantile Sexuality"

You can always polish the title later, once you have finished your literature search, read what you found, and have a better sense of the topic. Here is another example of shaping a topic for a one-semester course. This time the assignment is for an empirical research project:

Unlimited Topic (Too Broad for a Term Project)
"Why Do Humans and Animals Yawn?"

Slightly Limited Topic
"When Do Humans Yawn?"

Adequately Limited Topic
"When Do Baboons in Zoos Yawn?"

(Incidentally, if this particular topic sounds interesting, you might begin by reading R. Baenninger's "Some Comparative Aspects of Yawning in *Betta splendens* [Siamese fighting fish], *Homo sapiens* [humans], *Panthera leo* [lions], and *Papio sphynx* [baboons]," *Journal of Comparative Psychology,* 1987, Vol. 101, pp. 349–354; and R. Baenninger, S. Binkley, and M. Baenninger's "Field Studies of Yawning and Activity in Humans," *Physiology and Behavior,* 1996, Vol. 59, pp. 421–425.)

If you are currently enrolled in a research methods course, your text probably discusses criteria for assessing the merits of hypotheses. A detailed discussion is beyond the scope of this manual, but we can mention three criteria:

- ◆ Your hypotheses should be grounded in credible ideas and facts. In other words, you must do a literature search to find out whether your hypotheses are consistent with accepted findings in the scientific literature. If they are not, then you will need to think about the inconsistencies and decide (with the help of the instructor) whether you really have a fresh insight or will need to develop some other hypotheses.
- ◆ You need to state your hypotheses in a precise and focused way. To ensure that you are using technical terms correctly, you can consult resources in the library (relevant encyclopedias and psychological dictionaries, for example). To ensure that your hypotheses are focused, you can consult your instructor, who will show you how to use the winnowing principle known as *Occam's razor* to cut away unwieldy words and ideas. This principle takes its name from William of Ockham, a 14th-century English scholastic philosopher and Franciscan, who was known to his fellow friars as "doctor invincibilis." Also called the *principle of parsimony,* Occam's razor is the scientific mantra that what can be explained on fewer principles or with fewer entities is explained needlessly by more.
- ◆ Your hypotheses and predictions must be falsifiable if they are incorrect. That is, hypotheses that are not refutable by any conceivable empirical means are considered unscientific. For example, the statement "All behavior is a product of the good and evil within us" does not qualify as a valid scientific hypothesis, because it is so vague and amorphous that it cannot be subjected to empirical jeopardy.

Knowing Your Audience and Topic

All professional writers know that they are writing for a particular audience. This knowledge helps them determine the tone and style of their work. Think of a journalist's report of a house fire and contrast it with a short story describing the same event. Knowing one's audience is no less important when the writer is a college student and the project is an essay or a research report. The main audience is your instructor. Should you have any questions about the instructor's grading criteria, find out what the criteria are before you start to work.

For example, in a course on research methods (designated as a "writing course"), one instructor's syllabus contained the following grading criteria for different parts of the finished report (the numbers in parentheses are percentages):

Abstract
    Informativeness (5)
Introduction
    Clarity of purpose (10)
    Literature review (10)
Method
    Adequacy of design (10)
    Quality and completeness of description (10)
Results
    Appropriateness and correctness of analysis (10)
    Use of tables or figures (5)
    Clarity of presentation (10)
Discussion
    Interpretation of results (10)
    Critique/future directions (10)
Miscellaneous
    Organization, style, references, etc. (5)
    Appendix (5)

This kind of information enabled the students to concentrate on different parts of the assignment in the same way that the instructor would concentrate on them when evaluating the reports. This information can also serve as a checklist for you to make sure that everything of importance is covered adequately in your finished report. Not every instructor provides such detailed information about grading, but this manual can help you compose your own refined checklist.

Cultivating a Sense of Understanding

Let us assume that you know what your main audience—your instructor—expects of you. Now you must try to develop more than a superficial understanding of your topic. The more you read about it and discuss your ideas with friends, the more you will begin to cultivate an intuitive understanding of the topic. In the next chapter we describe how to use library and computerized resources to nurture this understanding. Here are three tips to get you started:

◆ Many writers find it helpful to keep several 3×5-inch cards handy, or to use sticky notes, for jotting down relevant ideas that suddenly occur to them. This is a good way to keep your subject squarely in your mind.

◆ You must also comprehend your source material, so equip yourself with a good desk dictionary, and turn to it routinely whenever you come across an unfamiliar word. It is a habit that will serve you well. The dictionary we recommend to students is *The American Heritage Dictionary of the English Language* (Houghton Mifflin), because it is lively, readable, and informative.

◆ While you shop for a dictionary, you might also buy a thesaurus. It can be useful as an index of terms in information retrieval (discussed in Chapter Two) as well as a treasury of synonyms and antonyms when you write.

Chapter Two

FINDING AND USING REFERENCE MATERIALS

The literature review is an essential step in writing a research report or an essay because it puts your paper in context and builds on previous work by others. Knowing about the many resources available in the library and knowing how to use them will allow you to gauge the effort it will take to do a literature review. If you know how to use them, recent technological advances can save you time and effort. This chapter shows you how to use traditional and innovative resources most effectively.

Using the Library

Let us assume you have an inkling of an idea for a writing or research project, have explored it in a very preliminary way with the instructor, and know that you must produce a written proposal. In the next chapter we will discuss the nature of the proposal for an essay topic or a research study. However, before you begin drafting your proposal, you will need to spend some time exploring your topic in the library. Later on, you will spend additional time in the library to gather the information you need to flesh out your final paper. So if you have never set foot in your college library, now is the time to get oriented.

You can ask at the Information Desk if there is a fact sheet (and floor plan) describing where to find things. But it is not convenient to return to the Information Desk every time you have a question, so you should be aware of other places you can turn for assistance. You will find that staff members (often called *information specialists*) are also available in specialized areas of the library. You should also find out where photocopiers are located and whether you need to bring coins or purchase a card in order to use them. It is a lot easier to photocopy a page from a journal or book than to copy lengthy passages by hand.

The Reference Desk is where you will find staff members who are true generalists and can answer all manner of questions or at least point you to sources that will help you answer them yourself. They may suggest reference works that are "not circulated" (cannot be checked out) but can be used in a specified section of the library. For example, if you wanted to find information about a particular test instrument, you would look in the *Mental Measurements Yearbook* for such information as the population for intended use, forms, cost, author, publisher, cross-references to earlier yearbooks, and references to critical authoritative reviews, journal articles, books, and dissertations that discuss the test. If you wanted material that was unavailable in your library, you would ask at the Reference Desk about an *interlibrary loan.*

Other important areas are the Circulation Desk, the Reserve Area, and the Current Periodicals Area. The Circulation Desk is where you check out books and other materials, return books, and take care of overdue notices. Bring an ID with you. The Reserve Area is for books, photocopies of journal articles, tests, and so on that your instructor has placed "on hold" or "on reserve" (not to be circulated). You can examine this material only in the library and for a specified period (for example, 2 hours). The Current Periodicals Area is where you find recent issues of journals, magazines, and newspapers. In some libraries (called *virtual libraries* or *digital libraries*), journals and periodicals (and maybe even books) can be perused electronically, a process that conserves space and prevents the problem of missing or damaged copies. Digital libraries share their resources through interconnected computers, so they expand the storehouse of available information.

To help you get further oriented, we will look over the shoulder of a student named Eric as he goes step by step through the process of doing a literature search. Eric is first interested in gathering sufficient background information to formulate a testable hypothesis and then write an acceptable proposal. But he thinks he will also have to do a more thorough search to accompany his final report. First, we describe the big picture; then, we examine the details of each resource used by Eric.

Looking Over Eric's Shoulder

Eric is at the stage of formulating a working hypothesis, and he thinks he wants to study a spin-off from the instructor's lecture on what she called the "Pygmalion effect," based on a classic study by Robert Rosenthal and Lenore Jacobson. In a book they wrote in 1968, called *Pygmalion in the Classroom,* Rosenthal and Jacobson described how, in the spring of 1964, they had given a standard nonverbal intelligence test to all the children in a public elementary school in South San Francisco. However, the teachers were told that the test was one of intellectual "blooming," and approximately 20% of the children (picked at random by the investigators) were represented to the teachers as capable of marked intellectual growth based on their performance on this test. In other words, the difference between the supposed potential bloomers and other students existed solely in the minds of their teachers. The children's performance on the intelligence test was then measured after one semester, again after a full academic year, and again after two full academic years. The results of this experiment revealed that, although the greatest differential gain in total intelligence appeared after 1 school year, the bloomers clearly held an advantage over the other children even after 2 years.

Eric's instructor described the phenomenon as an example of what are called *expectancy effects* in social psychology, and Eric thinks he might be interested in studying it further. First, he looks up the Rosenthal and Jacobson book in the library's card catalog, then locates the book in the stacks and peruses it for possible additional leads, paying particular attention to the list of references to see what sources the book's authors found helpful. While he is in the library, he also takes 20 minutes or so to look up the key term *expectancy effect* in several dictionaries of psychology that are handy. He finds that expectancy effects are also referred to as *experimenter expectancy effects,* and sometimes *Rosenthal effects,* because Rosenthal did so much landmark research on the topic. Eric notes these synonyms for key concepts so that he can use them when he searches the electronic databases later on.

Looking up terms in a psychological dictionary is an easy way to begin, and because Eric is new to the field of psychology, the synonyms and cross-references are helpful. Encyclopedias of psychology can also be very helpful, and most college libraries have several of these in their collections. As encyclopedias of psychology are usually near each other on the shelves, Eric asks a librarian for their location. He could also have looked up the call number for one encyclopedia of psychology and then scanned the shelves when he got into the stacks. He reads the encyclopedia entries to gain an understanding of the basic topic. All of Eric's work so far—using the card catalog, going to the stacks, finding the books, making notes—has taken him about an hour.

The next step is to use a computer to consult an electronic database, and Eric's library has computers that are specifically programmed to do this. Having previously done the simple search for a single title, author, or subject at the library's main catalog screen to get a call number, he has mastered about all the skills it will take to get through a database search. The difference is that the electronic database will allow him to customize the information that comes up on the screen, although if he wants, he can simply use the default screen. Each icon (or button) does something useful, and there is a HELP button if he is not sure. Eric's teacher recommended that he start with an electronic database called PsycLIT, which most colleges let students use in the library or through a modem connection using a browser.

Eric clicks on the PsycLIT site and checks off the years in which he is interested. Since all he is interested in is drumming up a good hypothesis, he feels he needs to check only the last 3 years. Without changing any of the fields that will be returned by the search, he just enters the first thing that comes into his head: "expect*" (no quote marks). The asterisk is like a wild card that tells the computer to search for any ending, such as "expects," "expecting," "expectancy," and "expectations." Eric gets 6,901 returns, far too many. He tries "expecta*" and gets 3,877, still too many. He tries "expectancy" and gets 639—better.

"Expectancy effects" gives him 22 returns—maybe too few, but maybe not. To find out for sure, he peruses the list to see what turned up.

There is a tiny box at the beginning of each record in the list that he can check for later printing or saving, or he can save the whole file without checking anything. Because he brought a blank disk with him, he saves the file on his disk. Saving the file can be a great time saver if the library printing station is very busy. Later on, he can edit the list and print it at his leisure (freeing up the library computer sooner, too). Eric notices how he can choose which fields show in each record, although he usually just selects "ALL" of them. He always includes the search history, thinking that he may need to replicate the search or may want to describe it in the Method section of his research report to show how he discovered his sources.

Electronic databases have their own "limited vocabularies," sets of words and phrases (called *descriptors*) regarding a topic. It is a good idea to explore these thoroughly; they are conveniently indexed in hypertext. PsycLIT refers to its set as a "Thesaurus." Eric clicks on this button and discovers a few more phrases to search with: "teacher expectations" returns 34; "teacher-student interaction," 499; and combining these two yields just 2 records. He checks out the 2 and then redisplays the list of 34 to save on his disk and peruse later. He tries a few more searches just for fun—and because they take only seconds to execute.

The SEARCHES button displays the history of Eric's search efforts, allowing easy review and also combining of search sets. He is astonished to see he has done 11 searches in a very short time. He happens to notice that he misspelled a word in one of his searches; when he corrects the spelling he gets three records instead of none. He wonders at the amazing flexibility and speed of the search engine. Just about anything he might want to do with the returned records he *can* do. He can sort the output by any field at all. If he were researching a particular author, for instance, he might find it useful to sort on the author's last name. Sorting on the source or year of publication could be handy in some situations as well. (Ask yourself what would be convenient for your purposes, and chances are the programmers have also thought of it and incorporated it.) So far, Eric has invested only a few hours at the library doing these initial searches, scanning and saving the relevant titles and abstracts to see if they are likely to help him.

Eric settles on an experimental design with three conditions, using 6 fellow students to be "teachers/perceivers" and 60 more to be "students/targets." The teachers will be asked to show their students how to construct a simple seven-piece puzzle into a given shape, and the solution will in fact be illustrated for the students while they execute the task. The teachers will be told that this is a coordination test, and that the students will be timed in accomplishing their solution. In one of the conditions, the teachers will also be told that some of their students—20 in all—have certain characteristics that have been correlated with "high coordination ability." In another condition, the teachers will be told that 20 other students have "low correlations with coordination." In the third condition, the remaining 20 students will be represented as "neither high nor low." Eric's hypothesis is that the "high-coordination" students will outperform the other two groups, and that the "low-correlations-with-coordination" students will underperform them.

In just a few hours, Eric has been able to do enough to get started on his project. Suppose he wants to extend the search. He has a lot of databases he can use, including one called ERIC (for Educational Resources Information Center). But his next step is to scan the contents of every *Annual Review of Psychology,* moving backward in time to the year after the seminal *Pygmalion in the Classroom* book in 1968. It takes him less than an hour to do this scan. Among the various references he finds is a milestone 1978 article in *Behavioral and Brain Sciences,* in which R. Rosenthal and D. B. Rubin describe a meta-analysis of the "first 345 studies" of expectancy effects. Unfortunately, the issue of the journal in which this article appeared is missing from his library. He looks up the abstract, finds that the article has 30 peer review comments and a reply by the authors, and decides he should order a copy through interlibrary loan. A bonus, he will find, is that the article also discusses a few rare disconfirming studies—one, like Eric's study, done in a lab involving teaching people to learn a game, a card trick in this case.

Encouraged by his discovery of the summary article in *Behavioral and Brain Sciences,* Eric wonders if there might be a more recent update of the work on interpersonal expectations. On the off chance that there might be a book by this title, he uses the Library of Congress on-line catalog to do a quick search for books with "interpersonal expectation" in the title. This search turns up several books, one of which looks particularly promising: *Interpersonal Expectations: Theory, Research and Applications,* edited by P. D. Blanck. Although the book is also listed in his library's card catalog, someone has borrowed it. Using PsycLIT, he looks up the chapter titles and contributors. Satisfied that the book is something he can really use, he orders it through interlibrary loan. Next, Eric asks a reference librarian for the location of the *Social Sciences Citation Index.* He looks for the summary volume of the most recent 6-month period, and under "R. Rosenthal," he looks up the recent citations of "68 Pygmalion Classroom." This search produces some reviews and a handful of articles. Following the manual trail of the reference lists of these articles, especially the reviews, will widen his search still further.

Eric's preliminary search turned up more than enough material to write his proposal, and it took only a few hours. If his project requires a more extensive search later, it may take many more hours, lengthening into days, as much of the reference and citation recording will have to be done by hand. He can also return to PsycLIT and include more years than in his earlier, preliminary search. Using the saved files from before, he can use the same search pattern (remember, he included the search histories in his output) to update the search from 1967 forward. If he does this, he will find a couple of hundred additional articles, which he can save to his disk and peruse when he has the time. All this work may not be something for a one-semester course, although it would be expected if he were doing a thesis or a dissertation. Before proceeding, Eric would do well to speak with his instructor to make sure the plan is realistic.

How Material Is Cataloged

Eric began his work by manually searching a catalog, called a *card catalog* (usually located near the Reference Desk), to find out where Rosenthal and Jacobson's *Pygmalion in the Classroom* was located in the library. The reason it is called a card catalog is that it consists of miles and miles of three types of alphabetized 3×5-inch index cards in file drawers: (a) author cards, (b) title cards, and (c) subject cards. If the card catalog no longer exists in your library, it is because it has been replaced by computers that contain an on-line or *automated catalog,* containing the same information that previously appeared on cards. If you have an Internet connection on your personal computer, you can do as Eric did and search the catalog of the Library of Congress in Washington, D.C., by going to http://lcweb.loc.gov/catalog. The Library of Congress cannot, of course, tell you whether the material you need is in your library's stacks, but using this site is an easy way to check a reference if you need the information right away. You will not have to enter a complete title, author, or subject; you can type in only a word, a last name, or a phrase. The computer will then help you find what you are looking for, and there are instructions and also a HELP button you can click on if you get confused.

The information you receive using the automated catalog might first appear in a slightly abbreviated form, giving only the author, title, publisher, and call number. When you ask for more on this record, what you will get is

EXHIBIT 3 *Sample catalog card*

<table>
<tr><td>LB
1131
R585</td><td>Rosenthal, Robert, 1933—
    Pygmalion in the classroom; teacher expectation and pupils'
intellectual development [by] Robert Rosenthal [and] Lenore
Jacobson. New York, Holt, Rinehart and Winston [1968]
      xi, 240 p. illus. 23 cm
      Bibliography: p. 219–229.</td></tr>
</table>

          1. Prediction of scholastic success. 2. Mental tests. I.
Jacobson, Lenore, joint author. II. Title.

LB1131.R585   372.1'2'644   68–19667

Library of Congress

similar to what appears in a card catalog. Exhibit 3 shows the catalog card for *Pygmalion in the Classroom,* the book that got Eric started. If your library still has a card catalog, this exhibit is what you will find if you look in the card file under either "Rosenthal, Robert" or "Jacobson, Lenore" (author card) or "Pygmalion in the classroom" (title card). The card shows a *call number:* a sequence of letters and numbers specified by the Library of Congress. The card also shows the name and birth date of the first author (Rosenthal, Robert, 1933–). Beneath are the title of the work and its subtitle ("teacher expectation and pupils' intellectual development"), followed by the complete list of authors in the order in which they appear on the title page of the work. Then follows the location and name of the publisher (New York, Holt, Rinehart and Winston) and the date of copyright (1968). The remainder of the card lists further technical details for librarians.

In case you are interested, the information in the middle of the card shows the number of prefatory pages (xi) and the length of the book (240 p.); it also indicates that the book contains figures or other illustrations (illus.), that it stands 23 cm. high on the shelf, and that the bibliography or list of references is on pages 219–229. The section below indicates the categories under which this book should be cataloged ("Mental tests," for example). Next is the book's Library of Congress classification number again (LB1131.R585), the Dewey decimal classification number of this work (372.1'2'644), the order number of this particular set of cards (68-19667), and from whom the cards can be ordered (Library of Congress).

Exhibit 4 shows the information Eric received by using the Library of Congress's on-line catalog. First, he was given an abbreviated record that simply listed the author, title, year of publication, and Library of Congress call number. Beneath the record was the notation "More on this record," which

EXHIBIT 4 Sample of on-line record at Library of Congress Web site

Title:	Interpersonal expectations : theory, research, and applications / edited by Peter David Blanck.
Published:	Cambridge [England] ; New York, NY, USA : Cambridge University Press ; Paris : Editions de la Maison des sciences de l'homme, 1993.
Description:	xviii, 500 p. : ill. ; 24 cm.
Series:	Studies in emotion and social interaction
LC Call No.:	BF323.E8I68 1993
Dewey No.:	158/.2 20
ISBN:	052141783X (hardback)
	0521428327 (pbk.)
	2735104923 (hardback : France only)
	2735104931 (pbk. : France only)
Notes:	Includes bibliographical references and indexes.
Subjects:	Expectation (Psychology)
	Interpersonal relations.
Other authors:	Blanck, Peter David, 1957-
Control No.:	92036925

Tagged display | Previous Record | Brief Record Display | New Search

Eric clicked to get the full record shown in Exhibit 4. The information in this exhibit is very similar to that in his library's card catalog.

The Library Stacks

The call number tells us where permanent material is stored in the stacks (the shelves throughout the library). The stacks are coded according to categories that coincide with the numbers and letters on the index card in the card catalog or the computer-readable catalog. For identification, the call number also appears at the bottom of the book's spine. To find Rosenthal and Jacobson's book, Exhibit 3 instructs us to go to the LB section of the stacks and, next, to the more specific section in numerical (1131) and then alphanumerical (R585) order where this book is shelved. If the material we want is not in the stacks, we can ask at the Reference Desk for help in locating it or, if the material is lost, for help in borrowing a copy through interlibrary loan. (Even though libraries cooperate in loaning books, it may take quite a while before we have the book in hand if our request has not been given a high priority by the lending library.)

Exhibit 5 shows the two systems of classification most frequently used in U.S. libraries. For psychology students, these systems may be puzzling because

EXHIBIT 5 Two systems of classification used in U.S. libraries

Library of Congress System		Dewey Decimal System	
A	General works	000	General works
B	Philosophy and religion	100	Philosophy
C	General history	200	Religion
D	Foreign history	300	Social sciences
E-F	America	400	Language
G	Geography and anthropology	500	Natural sciences
H	Social sciences	600	Technology
J	Political science	700	Fine arts
K	Law	800	Literature
L	Education	900	History and geography
M	Music		
N	Fine arts		
P	Language and literature		
Q	Science		
R	Medicine		
S	Agriculture		
T	Technology		
U	Military science		
V	Naval science		
Z	Bibliography and library science		

psychological material is classified under several different headings. The Library of Congress system divides material into 20 major groups, and abnormal psychology books, for example, can be found under BF or RC. The Dewey decimal system classifies material under 10 headings (and abnormal psychology can be found in the 157 class).

Some libraries attempt to protect their collection of books and journals by restricting access to the stacks. If you find yourself unable to access the stacks directly, you submit a form that lists the material you want to use, and a staff member then retrieves the material for you. However, if you are allowed to browse in the stacks, refer to Exhibit 6. It shows the cataloging of

EXHIBIT 6 Cataloging of psychological materials in U.S. libraries

Library of Congress System		Dewey Decimal System	
BF	Abnormal psychology	00-	Artificial intelligence
	Child psychology	13-	Parapsychology
	Cognition	15-	Abnormal psychology
	Comparative psychology		Child psychology
	Environmental psychology		Cognitive psychology
	Motivation		Comparative psychology
	Parapsychology		Environmental psychology
	Perception		Industrial psychology
	Personality		Motivation
	Physiological psychology		Perception
	Psycholinguistics		Personality
	Psychological statistics		Physiological psychology
HF	Industrial psychology	30-	Family
	Personnel management		Psychology of women
HM	Social psychology		Social psychology
HQ	Family	37-	Educational psychology
	Psychology of women		Special education
LB	Educational psychology	40-	Psycholinguistics
LC	Special education	51-	Statistics
Q	Artificial intelligence	61-	Psychiatry
	Physiological psychology		Psychotherapy
QA	Mathematical statistics	65-	Personnel management
RC	Abnormal psychology		
	Psychiatry		
	Psychotherapy		
T	Personnel management		

more specific areas by both systems. Browsing can lead you to a valuable but unexpected book or to a pertinent quote to illustrate some idea or point.

Using Reference Sources

Eric looked in dictionaries and encyclopedias of psychology. Finding one encyclopedia in the stacks, he then browsed for other relevant references shelved nearby. If you want the best unabridged dictionary of the English language, ask at the Reference Desk where to find the multivolume *Oxford English Dictionary* (called for short the *OED*). If you have the time and are interested in word origins, you will find the *OED* a fascinating resource to thumb through. Its purpose is to give the history of all words in the English language from the year A.D. 1150 to the publication of the *OED*. There is an abridged edition in two volumes (also published by the Oxford University Press), but you need a magnifying glass to read it. Some words in the *OED* have very different meanings today from their original meanings, and it can be psychologically informative to learn about these changes in meaning.

For example, if you are interested in gossip, look up the word *gossip* in the *OED,* and you will find that it did not always have a derisive or sexist connotation. It began as *god-sibbs,* for "godparents," meaning those with spiritual affinity to the person being baptized. Christenings were occasions for distant relatives to be present, leading to much small talk. In the same way that the *d* in *God's spell* was dropped to form *gospel, god-sibbs* led to *gossip.* Later on, the term came to imply a woman of light and trifling character who engaged in "idle talk." Current popular usage emphasizes that gossip is small talk or idle talk, usually by women, typically focusing on someone else's private or intimate relations. If this etymology has whetted your interest in this topic, you can do a quick search of the literature on the psychology of gossip using PsycLIT or PsycINFO.

As Exhibit 7 indicates, PsycINFO is the American Psychological Association's (APA) parent database of PsycLIT. As we describe in a moment, the database in your college library may be PsycLIT or PsycINFO; they are similar enough so that, for convenience and simplicity, we discuss them together. If you happen to check out some of the other databases in Exhibit 7, you will find that some references appear on more than one system. For example, PsycLIT contains some references that appear in the automated Social Work Abstracts and Sociological Abstracts. The print version of PsycLIT is called *Psychological Abstracts* (described in a moment), but there is not an exact correspondence between the two databases. As a librarian friend told us, the advantage of a computer-readable database is that patrons can search to their hearts' content. Libraries that have these automated systems usually have a bank of computers reserved for patrons, although you will probably have to wait your turn to use one. You might ask in your department or at the Reference Desk of the library whether there are computers in other locations that will allow you to communicate with the automated system through a modem,

EXHIBIT 7 *Sample of reference databases available on computers*

Name	*Coverage*
ABI/Inform	Business and personnel management, finance, consumer information, advertising.
Ask ERIC	Research reports, conference papers, teaching guides, books, and journal articles in education from preschool to the doctoral level; ERIC is an acronym for Educational Resources Information Center.
Census Lookup	Produced by the U.S. Census Bureau; offers access to data tables for specific types of geographic areas.
CQ Library	Web access to *CQ Weekly* and *CQ Researcher,* which provide legislative news about what is happening on Capitol Hill.
Current Contents	Contents of journals in psychology, education, philosophy, political science, law, and other areas.
Dissertation Abstracts Online	Abstracts of doctoral dissertations and theses in the United States and abroad.
EDGAR	Acronym for Electronic Data Gathering, Analysis, and Retrieval System, this is the Securities and Exchange Commission's database of electronic filings.
eHRAF	Acronym for Human Relations Area Files, this nonprofit institution at Yale University is a consortium of educational, research, cultural, and government agencies that provides ethnographic and related information by culture and subject.
GPO Access	U.S. Government Printing Office publications.
MathSciNet	Research literature in mathematics, with emphasis on data in *Mathematical Reviews* and *Current Mathematical Publications.*

and whether you can do a search using PsycLIT (or PsycINFO) using your personal computer.

As Exhibit 7 implies, there are research databases for just about every discipline and area of interest. Other examples include the *Abridged Index Medicus, Art Index, Biological Abstracts, Book Review Digest, Britannica Online, Film Index International, MLA* (Modern Language Association) *International Bibliography, Music Index, Philosopher's Index,* and *World Almanacs.* Our librarian friend suggests making a checklist of sources already searched, so that you do not backtrack without realizing it; list the abstract or index, the years searched, and the search terms that you used. However, do not simply make a citation list of dozens of articles you found, because your instructor will wonder if you have even read the work cited. Read the original work.

Eric also mentioned scanning the contents of the *Annual Review of Psychology,* which is a serial publication (that is, published at regular intervals). *Annual Reviews* consist of detailed review/synthesis articles by leading authorities on specialized topics, and looking in the reference section of an *Annual Review* article (as Eric did) is a good way to find key studies. Some

EXHIBIT 7 (*continued*)

Name	Coverage
MEDLINE	National and international references to millions of articles in medicine, biomedicine, and related fields.
NCJRS Database	The National Criminal Justice Reference Service database, which includes summaries of publications on criminal justice.
NTIS	U.S. Government reports of federally-sponsored research in societal behavior (e.g., attitudes), public policy, personnel, management, and other areas (such as engineering, agriculture, physics, and biology).
ProQuest	Access to scholarly journals, periodicals, newspapers, and magazines in the University of Michigan archives, including charts, maps, photos, and some literature in full-text format.
PsycINFO	The American Psychological Association's (APA) main database and the parent file of PsycLIT; PsycINFO has every record created by the APA back to 1887 in all areas of psychology.
PsycLIT	A large subset of PsycINFO, but does not include dissertations and technical reports.
Social Scisearch	*Social Sciences Citation Index (SSCI)* is the parent source of titles of works and names of authors.
Social Work Abstracts	Social work references; includes substance abuse, family, and mental health literature.
Sociological Abstracts	Sociological literature, including overlap with PsycLIT and Social Work Abstracts.

journals also specialize in integrative reviews, such as the *Psychological Bulletin* (a bimonthly publication of the APA) and the more recently inaugurated *Review of General Psychology* (a quarterly journal of the APA's Division of General Psychology). *Psychological Review* (a quarterly APA journal) and *Behavioral and Brain Sciences* (a quarterly published by Cambridge University Press) are other excellent sources of integrative articles. It was in *Behavioral and Brain Sciences* that Eric found the "milestone 1978 article" he needed, and there is a special section after each article (called "Open Peer Commentary") where you will find lively commentary on the article by other researchers. If you would like to see a listing and description of hundreds of journals that publish work in psychology, get the latest edition of *Journals in Psychology* (also published by APA).

A great many other useful dictionaries and reference sources are also usually available. For example, slang dictionaries will tell you the history of terms such as *hot dog* and *meathead*. They also provide information on rhyming slang, African-American slang, pig Latin, and so forth. If you are interested in information about people in the news or other prominent people, you can look in *Current Biography* or *Who's Who*. If you want to know about famous Americans from the past, you can look in the *Dictionary of American Biography* or *Who Was Who in America*. The *Dictionary of National Biography* tells about men and women in British history. Librarians can point you to other works that you may find useful. Our librarian friend reminds us to emphasize that librarians are highly skilled in helping students find material. No matter how busy the librarian looks, students should not be intimidated. Do not be afraid to approach a librarian for help in finding resource material, because that is the librarian's main purpose.

PsycINFO, PsycLIT, and Psychological Abstracts

The names PsycINFO and PsycLIT can get awfully confusing. Think of PsycINFO as the parent file of PsycLIT, but PsycINFO is also the name of a department at the American Psychological Association. Fortunately, the basic rules for using PsycINFO and PsycLIT databases are quite similar. If you are interested, the difference between them is that PsycLIT does not include dissertation abstracts or technical reports. PsycLIT is also in a CD-ROM format that your library receives quarterly, and PsycINFO is a commercial service leased to your library and updated monthly. To complicate matters, there is another subset of the PsycINFO database that is called PsycFIRST, used mainly at small colleges. PsycFIRST includes all the PsycINFO material, but only for the most recent three years and the current year. The print version of the journal, chapter, book, and technical report summaries that are accessible on these electronic databases is called *Psychological Abstracts,* and we will start with it because it will introduce you to the way that this information is abstracted and archived by the APA.

In Exhibit 8 you will see how abstracts (synopses) appear in *Psychological Abstracts*. These four abstracts are from a volume of *Psychological Abstracts* published in 1993: (a) an article by Anastasi (in a European journal) on the history of differential psychology; (b) a book by Spiegelman on Judaism and Jungian psychology; (c) a chapter by Foster and Brizius on women's issues; and (d) a journal article by Draper on working conditions and industrial safety. Notice that each abstract contains information about the particular work; it is essentially the same information you will find using PsycINFO or PsycLIT.

For instance, Anastasi's abstract begins with an accession number (27890), so you can find the abstract again by going back to this volume and looking up the accession number. The author's name is then listed; if there were more than four authors, the fourth would be followed by *et al.* ("and others"). The first author's affiliation is given next, and then the work's title is shown, followed by the journal (or other source) in which the work appeared. If the work was based on some previously published entry in *Psychological Abstracts,* that information appears next. A synopsis of the work

EXHIBIT 8 *Sample abstracts from Psychological Abstracts*

27890. **Anastasi, Anne.** (Fordham U, NY) **The differential orientation in psychology.** *Zeitschrift für Differentielle und Diagnostische Psychologie*, 1992 (Sep), Vol 13(3), 133–138. — Traces the development of differential psychology from a loosely joined bundle of topics, through an integrated field of psychology, to a distinct orientation toward all psychology. The differential orientation is characterized by (1) the recognition and measurement of variability as a fundamental property of all behavior and (2) the comparative analysis of behavior under varying environmental and biological conditions, as 1 approach to understanding the nature and sources of behavior. Major orienting concepts that can be widely applied within general psychology include the multiplicity and interaction of variables involved in behavioral effects, the overlapping of distributions, the multidimensionality of individual and group differences, and the development of individuality in relation to multiple group membership. (German abstract)

29177. **Spiegelman, J. Marvin. Judaism and Jungian psychology.** University Press of America: Lanham, MD, 1993, xi, 156 pp. ISBN 0-8191-8895-6 (hardcover).
TABLE OF CONTENTS
Introduction • Part I: Harmony • Jewish psychoecumenism (Univ. of Judaism, 1989) • A Jewish psychotherapist looks at the religious function of the psyche (Association of Orthodox Jewish Scientists, UCLA, 1989) • Struggling with the image of God (Cedars-Sinai Conference on Psychology and Judaism 1986) • Judaism and Jungian psychology: A personal experience • Part II: Disharmony • The Jewish understanding of evil in the light of Jung's psychology (1988) • Part III: Harmony and disharmony together • Julia, the atheist-communist • The medium, Sophie-Sarah [*from the publicity materials*] There has been a significant amount of commentary about the Jung who was, on the one hand, thought to harbor anti-Semitic sentiment and, on the other hand, a friend and teacher of many Jews. His school of psychology has had a large Jewish following throughout the world, including Israel. J. Marvin Spiegelman uses the works of C. G. Jung to foster a dialogue between Judaism and Christianity. He demonstrates the parallels between Jung's thought and classic Kabbalistic views on the masculine and feminine aspects of Divinity and all life; "Judaism and Jungian Psychology" supplements the work of Martin Buber and Eric Fromm in

this area of Biblical research. Spiegelman includes some of his own fiction, psychomythological in theme, from "The Tree."

29291. **Foster, Susan E. & Brizius, Jack A.** (Brizius & Foster, Private Consultant). **Caring too much? American women and the nation's caregiving crisis.** [In: (PA Vol 80:29128) *Women on the front lines: Meeting the challenge of an aging America.* Allen, Jessie & Pifer, Alan (Eds.). Urban Institute Press: Washington, DC, 1993. xv. 270 pp. ISBN 0-87766-574-5 (hardcover); 0-87766-575-3 (paperback).] pp. 47–73.
[from the chapter]
— as America's caregivers, women hold the family together and maintain the social structure of the country ◊ the combination of increased survival rates, lower mortality at very old ages, and women's increased labor force participation means that caregiving is no longer a potentially satisfying, if, burdensome, way of life but, instead, a crisis for an expanding proportion of women in America ◊ explores the dimensions of that crisis and examines ways in which public policy might be formulated to alleviate at least part of the burden of caregiving, which is sure to increase in the near future as our population ages.

31608. **Draper, Elaine.** (U Southern California, Los Angeles) **Fetal exclusion policies and gendered construction of suitable work.** Special Issue: Environmental justice. *Social Problems*, 1993(Feb), Vol 40(1), 90–107. —Examines fetal exclusion policies (FEPs) and argues against employers' claims that scientific research supports their definition of unacceptable risk used to exclude women from jobs requiring exposure to toxic substances. Definitions of acceptable risk in FEPs are not scientific or value-neutral, but are in fact socially constructed, and therefore reflect gender stratification, corporate control, and the culturally privileged position of the fetus. This is evident in 3 of these policies' effects: (1) They exclude only certain fertile women, not all workers at risk; (2) they give priority to fetal rights, at the expense of workers' rights; and (3) corporations see them as the least costly defense against damage suits. Also examined is problematic free choice rhetoric pervading the US Supreme Court case regarding the Johnson Controls Corporation's FEP. Conceptions and power relationships that underlie fetal exclusion are also discussed.

follows; next are the number of references and the source of the abstract. The "German abstract" in parentheses tells us that the synopsis appears in a different language from that of the original work.

The abstract of Spiegelman's book shows the table of contents and contains a note indicating that the synopsis is from publicity material supplied by the publisher. It also shows the name and location of the publisher, the copyright date, the number of prefatory pages, the length of the book, and a unique code assigned by the publisher that identifies this edition of the book (the ISBN, or International Standard Book Number). The abstract of the chapter by Foster and Brizius contains parenthetical information about the book in which it appeared and notes that the book was previously indexed in *Psychological Abstracts*. An open diamond (◊) is used to separate a quoted phrase.

A computer search using PsycLIT or PsycINFO is faster and more fun than doing a hand search of *Psychological Abstracts*. All you need to get started is a question that you want to answer and some descriptors. Eric began by searching for material on "teacher expectations" and "teacher-student interactions" and then combined these two descriptors. He also looked in PsycLIT's "Thesaurus" to find related descriptors that were indexed in the system. Exhibit 9 shows what he pulled up about Rosenthal and Rubin's *Behavioral and Brain Sciences* article, and Exhibit 10 shows what he received about P. D. Blanck's *Interpersonal Expectations* book. If the system your library subscribes to is based on Windows, you may be asked to check boxes to indicate the type of search you are requesting, for example, "☐Journal Articles[and period]" or "☐PsycINFO Chapter Records" or "☐PsycINFO Book Records." However, the newest Windows systems now combine journal, chapter, and book databases so that no "check boxes" are necessary. Or you can do a "Quick Search" of words in any field, or a "Field Restricted Search" that limits the search to specified authors, sources, keywords, and so on. Once you have pulled up a set of records, you can SAVE them as a file on your disk and peruse them when you have time, PRINT them, or even E-mail them to yourself if you forgot to bring a disk with you.

Social Sciences Citation Index

One of the reference databases listed in Exhibit 7 is Social Scisearch, which is based on the *Social Sciences Citation Index (SSCI)*, published by the Institute for Scientific Information. Eric looked in the most recent 6-month summary volume of *SSCI* to find current citations of *Pygmalion in the Classroom*. The printed version of the *SSCI* is not difficult to use if the computerized version is unavailable. This continuously updated database consists of three separate but related indexes to the behavioral and social science literature as far back as 1966. The printed form of *SSCI* shows—in alphabetical order, by the last name of the first author—the year's published literature that cited the work. So Eric looked up "Robert Rosenthal" and "*Pygmalion in the Classroom*" to find a list of reviews and articles that helped him widen his search. Since libraries

EXHIBIT 9 PsycINFO *abstract of journal article*

Accession Number
     1980-26766-001
Author
     Rosenthal, Robert; Rubin, Donald B.
Affiliation
     Harvard U
Title
     Interpersonal expectancy effects: The first 345 studies.
Source
     Behavioral & Brain Sciences. 1978 Sep Vol 1(3) *377-415*
ISSN/ISBN
     0140-525X
Language
     English
Abstract
     The research area of interpersonal expectancy effects originally derived from
consideration of the effects of experimenters on the results of their research. One of these is
the expectancy effect, the tendency for experimenters (Es) to obtain results they expect, not
simply because they have correctly anticipated nature's response but rather because they
helped to shape that response through their expectations. In recent years, the research has
been extended from Es to teachers, employers, and therapists whose expectations for their
pupils, employees, and patients might also come to serve as interpersonal self-fulfilling
prophecies. The results of 345 experiments investigating interpersonal expectancy effects are
summarized. These studies fall into 8 broad categories of research: reaction time, inkblot tests,
animal learning, laboratory interviews, psychophysical judgments, learning and ability, person
perception, and everyday life situations. For the entire sample of studies, as well as for each
specific research area (a) the overall probability that interpersonal expectancy effects do in
fact occur is determined, (b) their average magnitude is estimated to evaluate their substantive
and methodological importance, and (c) methods that may be useful to others wishing to
summarize quantitatively entire bodies of research are illustrated. 30 peer comments and a
reply by the authors are included. (50 ref) ((c) 1999 APA/PsycINFO, all rights reserved)
Key Phrase Identifiers
     interpersonal expectancy effects & E bias in psychological research, peer comments &
authors' reply
Keywords (Thesaurus Terms)
     Experimental Methods; Experimenter Bias; Experimenter Expectations; Professional
Criticism; Professional Contribution; Professional Criticism Reply
Classification Codes
     2260 Research Methods & Experimental Design
Population
     10 Human
Population Location
Form/Content Type
     1300 Literature Review/Research Review; 0500 Comment
Table of Contents (Book Records only)
Publication Year
     1978

EXHIBIT 10 PsycINFO *abstract of edited book*

Accession Number
    1994-97010-000
Author
    Blanck, Peter David (Ed)
Affiliation
    U Iowa, Coll of Law, Iowa City, IA, USA
Title
    Interpersonal expectations: Theory, research, and applications.
Source
    New York, NY, USA: Cambridge University Press; Paris, France: Editions De La
Maison Des Sciences De L'Homme (1993) xviii, 500 pp.
ISSN/ISBN
    0-521-41783 -X (hardcover); 0-52 1-42832-7 (paperback)
Language
    English
Abstract
    (from the preface) This volume provides innovative and critical reviews of the study
of interpersonal expectations in three basic areas: (1) real-world applications of research on
interpersonal expectations, (2) exploration of the mediation of interpersonal expectations
through verbal and nonverbal behavior, and (3) discussion of emerging statistical and
methodological techniques for understanding and studying interpersonal expectations. ((c)
1999 APA/PsycINFO, all rights reserved)
Key Phrase Identifiers
    interpersonal expectations theory & research methodology & applications &
mediation through verbal & nonverbal behavior
Keywords (Thesaurus Terms)
    Expectations; Interpersonal Interaction; Experimentation; Methodology; Nonverbal
Communication; Verbal Communication
Classification Codes
    3020 Group & Interpersonal Processes
Population
    10 Human
Population Location
Form/Content Type
Table of Contents (Book Records only)

```
Preface
List of contributors
Introduction
Interpersonal expectations: Some antecedents and some consequences
Robert Rosenthal
Systematic errors to be expected of the social scientist on the basis
of a general psychology of cognitive bias
Donald T. Campbell
Part I: Research on interpersonal expectations
Introduction to research on interpersonal expectations,
John M. Darley and Kathryn C. Oleson
Interpersonal expectations in the courtroom: Studying judges' and
juries' behavior
Peter David Blanck
Expectancies and the perpetuation of racial inequity
Marylee C. Taylor
Pygmalion--25 years after interpersonal expectations in the classroom
```

EXHIBIT 10 *continued*

Elisha Babad
Interpersonal expectations in organizations
Dov Eden
Interpersonal expectations and the maintenance of health
Howard S. Friedman
Precursors of interpersonal expectations: The vocal and physical
attractiveness stereotypes
Miron Zuckerman, Holley S. Hodgins and Kunitate Miyake
In search of a social fact: A commentary on the study of interpersonal
expectations
Harris Cooper
Part II: Research on the mediation of interpersonal expectations
through nonverbal behavior
The spontaneous communication of interpersonal expectations
Ross Buck
The accurate perception of nonverbal behavior: Questions of theory and
research design
Dane Archer, Robin Akert and Mark Costanzo
Nonverbal communication of expectancy effects: Can we communicate high
expectations if only we try?
Bella M. DePaulo
Gender, nonverbal behavior, and expectations
Judith A. Hall and Nancy J. Briton
Expectations in the physician-patient relationship: Implications for
patient adherence to medical treatment recommendations
M. Robin DiMatteo
Comment: Interpersonal expectations, social influence, and emotional
transfer
Klaus R. Scherer
Part III: The study of interpersonal expectations
The methodological imagination: Insoluble problems or investigable
questions?
Dane Archer
Issues in studying the mediation of expectancy effects: A taxonomy of
expectancy situations
Monica J. Harris
Analysis of variance in the study of interpersonal expectations:
Theory testing, interaction effects, and effect sizes
Frank J. Bernieri
Statistical tools for meta-analysis: From straightforward to esoteric
Donald B. Rubin
The volunteer problem revisited
Ralph L. Rosnow
Assessment and prevention of expectancy effects in community mental
health studies
Mary Aznanda Dew
Comment: Never-ending nets of moderators and mediators
Marylee C. Taylor
Author index
Subject index

Publication Year
    1993

EXHIBIT 11 SSCI citations of Pygmalion in the Classroom

68 Pygmalion Classroom

Ambady N	Psychol B	111	256	92	R
Aronson JM	J Exp S Psy	28	277	92	
Berliner DC	Educ Psych	27	143	92	
Carnelle KB	J Soc Pers	9	5	92	
Deci EL	Educ Psych	26	325	91	
Ensminge ME	Sociol Educ	65	95	92	
Epstein EH	Ox Rev Educ	18	201	92	
Feingold A	Psychol B	111	304	92	R
Gaynor JLR	J Creat Beh	26	108	92	
Goldenbe C	Am Educ Res	29	517	92	
Haring KA	T Ear Child	12	151	92	
Jussim L	J Pers Soc	62	402	92	
"	"	63	947	92	
Kershaw T	J Black St	23	152	92	
Kravetz S	Res Dev Dis	13	145	92	
Mayes LC	J Am Med A	267	406	92	
McDiarmi GW	J Teach Edu	43	83	92	
McGorry PD	Aust Nz J P	26	3	92	R
Milich R	Sch Psych R	21	400	92	
Musser LM	Bas Appl Ps	12	441	91	
Schwartz CA	Library Q	62	123	92	R
Semmel MI	J Spec Educ	25	415	92	
Spangenb ER	J Publ Pol	11	26	92	
Suen HK	T Ear Child	12	66	92	

Source: Reprinted from the *Social Sciences Citation Index,* ® Year 1992, Volume 3, with the permission of the Institute for Scientific Information® (ISI), © copyright 1992.

usually keep many back volumes of *SSCI,* he could have done an *ancestry search* by tracking down all relevant citations going back every 6 months.

To illustrate, when we looked up "Robert Rosenthal" and then listed under his name the book *"Pygmalion in the Classroom"* in the 1992 *SSCI,* we found the list of entries shown in Exhibit 11. Each entry gives the author of a work that refers to this book (for example, Ambady, N.), the source of the work (*Psychological Bulletin*), the volume number (111), the beginning page number (256), the year of publication (1992), and, in this case, a code letter (*R*) designating that the work was a review of the literature. Other code letters used by the *SSCI* are *C* for corrections; *D* for discussions (conference items); *L* for letters; *M* for meeting abstracts; *N* for technical notes; *RP* for reprint; and *W* for computer reviews (hardware, software, and database reviews). If there is no code letter, it means that the work is an article, report, technical paper, or the like. There is a companion index to the *SSCI* called the *Science Citation Index (SCI),* which is usually next to the *SSCI* in the stacks, so it might pay you to look in both indexes if you are doing an exhaustive search for a bibliography (that is, a complete list of readings).

We mentioned how Eric used the *SSCI* and Social Scisearch to do a search, but another example may be helpful for students who are preparing a bibliography. For his MA thesis, another student was interested in people who volunteer and then fail to show up for research participation, also called *pseudovolunteers* or *no-shows.* He first searched some standard databases, including PsycLIT, ABI/Inform, MEDLINE, ERIC, and Dissertation Abstracts Online. He then consulted the *Social Sciences Citation Index* because he thought that people who wrote about pseudovolunteering might have cited a 1975 book, *The Volunteer Subject,* that provides a definitive discussion of this topic. He developed a bibliography of over 200 publications that had cited this book and then pared this list to only those publications that were relevant to pseudovolunteering. He had to read all the relevant articles in order to extract the basic quantitative data he needed for his thesis. This was a more exhaustive search than is necessary for a course paper, but it is not unusual for a bibliography for a graduate research project.

The Fugitive Literature

Work that is unpublished, or perhaps hard to find (before the days of electronic databases such as those in Exhibit 7), is termed the *fugitive literature* (or *gray literature*). For a detailed discussion of this subject, read M. C. Rosenthal's chapter, "The Fugitive Literature," in H. Cooper and L. V. Hedges's *Handbook of Research Synthesis* (Russell Sage, 1994, pp. 85–94). For example, certain private institutions and government agencies support research that may be circulated only in technical reports. Other examples of the fugitive literature include unpublished papers that are presented at professional meetings, as well as dissertations and theses that graduate students write. If the work you are seeking is in the interlibrary loan network, you can request that your library borrow it, but be prepared for a long wait.

If your library subscribes to a variety of research databases, you may find what you are looking for on-line, including conference proceedings, government reports, and the like. If you have the time to spare, you can write to the author for the needed material or request follow-up studies if you are familiar with the author's previous work and suspect there may be more work in an unpublished form (for example, talks and technical reports). You will increase the likelihood of obtaining a response if your request is precise and convincing. Researchers receive many requests for reprints (printed copies or photocopies of published articles), preprints (copies of manuscripts in press), and other information, so do not expect a busy researcher to answer a long line of questions or to send you material that is readily available in any college library.

If you are in a department that has many active researchers on the staff, it is possible that one of them is working on the very problem that interests you. To find out, ask your instructor, and also ask if it will be OK to approach that person. If the answer is yes, set up an appointment to discuss your interests, but be sure to do your homework on the subject first. List for yourself the questions you want to ask, and then take notes during the interview. You may be able to make a connection through the Internet with someone who knows something, but simply surfing the Net can be a real time waster. For tips on how to use the Internet more efficiently to track down relevant material, see the latest edition of A. T. Stull's *Psychology on the Internet* (Prentice Hall) and E. P. Kardas's *Psychology Resources on the World Wide Web* (Brooks/Cole).

Taking Notes in the Library

We have discussed locating material but not taking notes in the library. If you have the funds, the best way to ensure that your notes will be exact is to photocopy the original material. But be sure to record in a conspicuous place on the photocopy the complete citation of all you copied. You will still need to interpret what you copied, and it is often easier to make notes of your interpretation at the time you have the material in hand. Having such notes will enable you to write an accurate paper as well as one that is efficiently organized.

Making detailed notes will also help you avoid committing *plagiarism* accidentally. We will have more to say about this subject in Chapter Six, but you plagiarize intentionally when you knowingly copy or summarize someone's work without acknowledging that source. You plagiarize accidentally when you copy someone's work but forget to credit it or to put it in quotation marks. Plagiarism is illegal, and you should guard against it by keeping accurate notes and giving full credit to others when it is due.

If you are taking extensive notes on a laptop computer, you need some way to distance yourself from pages and pages of notes in order to make them coherent. The same would be true if you were taking handwritten notes in the library. A useful strategy with handwritten notes is to use a separate index card for each quotable idea that you find as you uncover relevant material in your literature search. Many writers prefer making notes on 5×8-inch index cards because they can usually get all the information they want on the front of a large card, so it's easier to find what they want later. If you are using a computer to take notes, print them out and then cluster them in logical batches (similar to using large index cards). For each note, be sure to include the full reference of the material, including all the information you will need for the References section of your paper, and the page numbers of verbatim quotes (to cite in the narrative of your paper).

If you have made an outline for an essay (as described in Chapter Four), you can code each card or printout with the particular section of the outline that the material on the card or printout will illustrate (or you can use color coding). An alternative is to use a folder for each section of your paper or report, and then to file the relevant batches in the appropriate folder. In this way you can maintain a general order in your notes and avoid facing a huge stack of miscellaneous bits and pieces of information that will loom large as you try to sort and integrate into a useful form all the information you find in the library. If you are using reference numbers to code your material, be consistent, because a haphazard arrangement will only slow you down when it is time to write the first draft.

The most fundamental rule of note taking is to be thorough and systematic so that you do not waste time and energy having to return to the same book or article. Because memory is porous, it is better to photocopy or record too much than to rely on recall to fill in the gaps. Be sure your notes will make sense to you when you examine them later.

Additional Tips

Here are some more tips to help you get started on the literature search and do it efficiently:

◆ Try to be realistic in assessing how many books and articles you will need in your literature review. Too few may result in a weak foundation for your project, but too much material and intemperate expectations may overwhelm you and your subject. You are writing not a doctoral dissertation or an article for publication in a journal but a required paper that must be completed within a limited amount of time.

◆ How can you find out what is a happy medium between too little and too much? Talk with your instructor before you start an intensive literature search. Ask whether your plan seems realistic.

◆ Before you start your literature search, ask the instructor to recommend any key works that you should read or consult. Even if you feel confident about your topic already, asking the instructor for specific leads can prevent your going off on a tangent.

◆ Do not expect to finish your literature search in one sitting. Students with unrealistic expectations make themselves overly anxious and rush a task that should be done patiently and methodically to achieve the best result.

◆ In planning your schedule, give yourself ample time to do a thorough job. Patience will pay off by making you feel more confident that you understand your topic well.

◆ Suppose you cannot locate the original work that you are looking for in the stacks. Some students return repeatedly to the library, day after

day, seeking a book or journal article before discovering that it has
been lost or stolen or is being rebound. Ask an information librarian
to find the elusive material. If the original work you need is unavailable, the librarian may consult another college library. However, the
material could take so long to arrive that you might miss the deadline
set by your instructor (which is not an acceptable excuse).

◆ If you are looking for a specialized work, you probably will not find it
in a small public library, so do not waste your time. When students
spend a lot of time off-campus in public libraries and bookstores looking for source material, they usually come back with references from
general texts or current mass-market books and periodicals, which are
rarely acceptable sources.

◆ Follow our librarian friend's advice: Keep a running checklist of
sources searched and the search terms you used so that you don't accidentally retrace your steps.

Library Etiquette

Before we turn to the basics of developing your proposal for an essay or a research report, here is some final advice about using your library. The golden
rule of library etiquette is to respect your library and remember that others
also have to use it:

◆ Be quiet.
◆ Never tear out pages of journals or books.
◆ Never write in library journals or books.
◆ Do not monopolize material or machines.
◆ Return books and periodicals as soon as you finish with them.

Chapter Three

DRAFTING THE PROPOSAL

*O*nce *you have chosen your topic and begun your library work, the next step is to develop a proposal of what you plan to do. Some instructors feel that a brief oral presentation of your plan is sufficient. Others require a written proposal as a way of ensuring that both the instructor and you have a common understanding of your topic and procedures.*

Purpose of the Proposal

The purpose of your proposal is to tell the instructor what you would like to study and to write about in your essay or research report. However, it is not simply a one-way agreement, but an opportunity for the instructor to provide feedback and to raise questions. If you are required to do an empirical study, the proposal is also an opportunity to address ethical issues before you are permitted to collect any data. The proposal thus serves as a kind of "letter of agreement," in which you and the instructor agree that the planned project is ethically sound and methodologically feasible, and that you will consult with the instructor before making any changes in the procedure agreed upon.

Instructors may require preliminary submissions in addition to a final proposal. They may also ask for details in addition to those illustrated in the sample proposals in this chapter. For example, some instructors ask that students tell how they arrived at their ideas and why they believe the topic they selected is interesting and important. The purpose of such questions is (a) to help you crystallize your ideas, (b) to encourage you to focus on a topic you find intrinsically interesting, and (c) to make sure that these are *your* ideas. We will have more to say about the third point in a later chapter, but it is essential that the work be your own even if it builds on, or is a replication of, previous work by others.

Incidentally, one reason why replication is universally regarded as an essential criterion of genuine scientific knowledge is that, without repeating experiments, scientists cannot continue the discovery process by clarifying and expanding the meaning and limits of their hypotheses. Someone once compared the scientist to a person trying to unlock a door using a hitherto untried key. The role of replication, we might say, is to make the key available to others so they can see for themselves whether or not the key works. It does not mean simply reproducing the identical p value, but observing a similar relationship or seeing the same phenomenon. Suppose you were out jogging one morning and spotted two Martians—not two people disguised as Martians, but real Martians: green skin, antennas poking out of their scalps, and all the rest. You are not going to whip out your calculator, but you sure are going to ask the nearest earthling, "Do you see what I see?" This is what replication in science is all about, to see for yourself what others have claimed to see. It is also why replications are often the basis of undergraduate theses or master's theses. However, the student is expected to add to the design some personal creative touch in the form of a new hypothesis or some innovative aspect.

The Essay Proposal

Exhibit 12 shows the basic structure of the proposal for an essay. The working title (which can be changed later) gives an overall preview of the topic you selected. You then discuss in more detail (although briefly) the objective of your essay; you need to explain very clearly where you are heading and why you decided to go in that direction. And finally, the last section tells the instructor how you plan to do the literature search to familiarize yourself with the work that has already been done on your chosen topic. The instructor's comments on your proposal will continue the process of shepherding you toward your final goal.

The Research Proposal

Exhibits 13 and 14 show the basic structure of the proposal for a research project. The aims of the two proposals are very different, but the basic structure is similar. Each proposal starts with a working title that gives a preview of the study. The student then discusses in detail the objective of the study and leads into the hypotheses. The proposed method comes next, and any instruments to be used would be described here. If you have developed a measure, it belongs here or in an accompanying appendix. Next described is the overall plan for analyzing the qualitative or quantitative data. Finally, the student defends the ethics of the proposed research.

Ethical Considerations

Ethical accountability is an important issue in psychology, particularly when one is conducting and reporting empirical research. Thus, your instructor may require that you answer very specific questions in your proposal regarding the

EXHIBIT 12 *Sample proposal for an essay*

Essay Proposal for (Course No.)

Submitted by Anne A. Skleder

(Date Submitted)

Working Title

A Comparison of Two Views of Intelligence: With Emphasis on Gardner's Theory

of Multiple Intelligences

Objective

My essay will compare the classic view of intelligence with a more current

view. The classic view is that there is a common factor in all measures of

intelligence (called the g factor); theories that are consistent with this "g-centric"

(i.e., g-centered) position have been dominant in psychology for many decades. In

contrast to the classic approach is what I will call the multiplex view, by which I

mean that many kinds of intelligences may be housed within the same culture (like

movies in a multiplex theater). My essay will focus on one prominent example of

this multiplex view, the theory that Howard Gardner has called multiple

intelligences. I will explain the nature of Gardner's theory and also discuss some

criticisms of it. I will try to give a flavor of what seems to be the direction of work in

the area of intelligence.

Literature Search Strategy

I have started to search research databases and will continue to search

PsycLIT, ERIC, and other databases that are available in my college library. I have

already found some key papers and will do an ancestry search using SSCI, using the

work of Robert Sternberg and Steven Ceci as my starting point. I also found

EXHIBIT 12 Continued

particularly useful an article that was written by a task force of the American Psychological Association (Neisser et al., 1996).

Preliminary List of References

Gardner, H. (1983). <u>Frames of mind: The theory of multiple intelligences.</u> New York: Basic Books.

Gilbert, H. B. (1971). Intelligence tests. In L. C. Deighton (Ed.), <u>The encyclopedia of education</u> (Vol. 5, pp. 128-135). New York: Macmillan and Free Press.

Neisser, U., Boodoo, G., Bouchard, T. J., Jr., Boykin, A. W., Brody, N., Ceci, S. J., Halpern, D. F., Loehlin, J. C., Perloff, R., Sternberg, R. J., & Urbina, S. (1996). Intelligence: Knowns and unknowns. <u>American Psychologist, 51,</u> 77-101.

Sternberg, R. J. (1997). The concept of intelligence and its role in lifelong learning and success. <u>American Psychologist, 52,</u> 1030-1037.

Thurstone, L. L. (1938). <u>Primary mental abilities.</u> Chicago: University of Chicago Press.

EXHIBIT 13 Sample proposal for an experimental study

Research Proposal for (Course No.)

Submitted by Bruce Rind

(Date Submitted)

Working Title

An Experimental Study of the Effects of a Small Gift on Tipping Responses

Objective

In a preliminary search of the literature, I came upon an interesting article in the Cornell Hotel and Restaurant Administration Quarterly, which noted various techniques that servers can use to improve their tipping percentages. Most of these techniques seem to involve boosting the customers' impressions of the server's friendliness (e.g., a friendly touch or drawing a smiling face on the check). I would like to experiment with another technique, in which the server will present customers with a small gift (chocolate candy). After reading an article that was suggested to me by the instructor, I became interested in whether reciprocity is a factor moderating the effectiveness of this technique. In that article, Regan (1971) described reciprocity as the idea that people feel obligated to return a favor received. I think that reciprocity can be manipulated by attributing the small gift either to the restaurant or to the generosity of the server.

I have three hypotheses. First, on the assumption that the gift will be perceived by customers as a gesture of friendliness, I hypothesize that the presentation of the gift will have the effect of increasing tips when compared with a no-gift control condition. Second, I hypothesize that this effect is cumulative (i.e., up to a certain point), so that offering more candies will increase tips even more.

EXHIBIT 13 *Continued*

Rind   2

Third, inspired by Regan's idea of reciprocity, I hypothesize that when customers are under the impression that the offer of a gift reflects the server's rather than the restaurant's generosity, there will be an increase in tips.

Proposed Method

    I have described my proposed study to the owner of an upscale Italian-American restaurant in central New Jersey and have gotten his permission, and I have also described the study to a female server, who has agreed to participate. I will use a randomized design with four groups: (a) no candy condition, (b) 1 piece of candy condition, (c) 2 pieces of candy condition, and (d) 1+1 piece condition. I will write the condition on a card, then shuffle all the cards and have the server draw one card at a time. There will be 20 cards for each condition, and thus the expected total $\underline{N}$ = 80 dining parties.

    One set of cards will state "1 piece," which means that the server is to offer each customer in the dining party one piece of candy of his or her choice when presenting the check. A second set of cards will state "2 pieces," which means the server is to offer each customer two pieces of candy when presenting the check. A third set of cards will state "1+1," which means the server is to offer the customer one candy when presenting the check but say, "Oh, have another piece," as if the second candy were an afterthought; this condition is intended to emphasize the server's (as opposed to the restaurant's) generosity. In the fourth (or zero control) condition, the server will simply present the check without any candy offer.

    The server's interaction with customers in the dining party will be limited to the presentation of the check and the prescribed treatment. When the dining parties

EXHIBIT 13 *Continued*

Rind   3

leave, the server will record on the same index card that was used to determine the experimental condition the amount of the tip left by the party, the amount of the bill before taxes, and the party size.

Proposed Data Analysis

The dependent measure will be defined as the tip percentage, that is, the amount of the tip divided by the amount of the bill before taxes, which will then be multiplied by 100. I will report descriptive data for the results, and I plan to use contrasts as described by Rosnow and Rosenthal (1996), which I should be able to do using a calculator. I will consult with the instructor about the lambda weights I need to test my three hypotheses.

Ethical Considerations

The study involves a mild deception in that the customers are unaware that they are participating in an experiment. However, I do not propose to debrief them because no potential risk is involved. I cannot ask the people who are dining whether they will agree to "participate in an experiment" because that would simply destroy the credibility of the manipulation and render the study scientifically meaningless. The server and the owner will be given full details of the results, and all tips will be the property of the server.

Preliminary List of References

Department of Commerce. (1990). Statistical abstracts of the United States. Washington, DC: Author.

Lynn, M. (1996). Seven ways to increase servers' tips. Cornell Hotel and Restaurant Administration Quarterly, 37(3), 24-29.

EXHIBIT 13 *Continued*

Rind   4

McCall, M., & Belmont, H. J. (1995). <u>Credit card insignia and tipping:</u> <u>Evidence for an associative link.</u> Unpublished manuscript, Ithaca College.

Regan, D. T. (1971). Effects of a favor and liking on compliance. <u>Journal of</u> <u>Experimental Social Psychology, 7,</u> 627-639.

Rosnow, R. L., & Rosenthal, R. (1996). Computing contrasts, effect sizes, and counternulls on other people's published data: General procedures for research consumers. <u>Psychological Methods, 1,</u> 331-340.

EXHIBIT 14 *Sample proposal for an archival study*

Research Proposal for (Course No.)

Submitted by Peter B. Crabb

(Date Submitted)

Working Title

The Nature of Representations of Work and Gender in High-Profile Books for

Children

Objective

Gender is an important factor determining the division of labor in

industrialized societies. I am interested in how high-profile books for children

portray work and gender, as I suspect that these portraits may reinforce gender

stereotypes (cf. Bussey & Perry, 1982; Gettys & Cann, 1981). I would like to do a

content analysis of a random sample of pictures depicting both work and gender in

children's books that have received the Newbery and Caldecott awards. I have two

hypotheses:

1. In comparison with male characters, female characters are more likely to be

shown doing household work.

2. In comparison with female characters, male characters are more likely to be

shown doing production work outside the home.

Proposed Method

In a preliminary search in the library, I found a number of books that describe the

method of content analysis. I will begin by photocopying illustrations that clearly

show both work and gender. Under the instructor's guidance, I will create a

representative sample of these illustrations. Two students have agreed to code the

EXHIBIT 14 *Continued*

illustrations for (a) what tool is shown in the picture, (b) what type of work is represented (i.e., household, production, or other), and (c) whether the person doing the work is male, female, or unidentifiable by gender. The coders will be told that "household work" means "the use of tools in and around the home to prepare food, to clean, and to care for family members." "Production work," they will be told, means "the use of tools outside the home for construction, agriculture, or transportation." And "other work" will be defined as "work that does not qualify as either household or production, including the use of tools for leisure activities and for protection from the elements."

Proposed Data Analysis

The instructor suggested that for my data analysis I consult Fleiss (1981) to learn how to compare percentages or proportions. I plan to quantify the interrater reliability of the coders using another procedure described in Fleiss. Since all these procedures are new to me, however, I will meet with the instructor to make sure that I am proceeding correctly. I will be doing the computations using a calculator, and I will show my results to the instructor before writing the final report.

Ethical Considerations

I believe there are no ethical problems in this research because the raw data are in the public domain, and they are also nonsensitive. I will give the coders a copy of my final report, and I will compensate each coder with a music tape or CD of that person's choice.

Preliminary List of References

Association for Library Service to Children. (1990). The Newbery and Caldecott awards. Chicago: American Library Association.

EXHIBIT 14 *Continued*

Crabb   3

Bussey, K., & Perry, D. G. (1982). Same-sex imitation: The avoidance of cross-sex models or the acceptance of same-sex models? <u>Sex Roles, 8,</u> 773-784.

Department of Labor. (1991). <u>Working women: A chartbook</u> (Bulletin 2385). Washington, DC: Bureau of Labor Statistics.

Elder, G. H., Jr., Pavalko, E. K., & Clipp, E. C. (1993). <u>Working with archival data: Studying lives.</u> Newbury Park, CA: Sage.

Fleiss, J. L. (1981). <u>Statistical methods for rates and proportions.</u> New York: Wiley.

Gettys, L. D., & Cann, A. (1981). Children's perceptions of occupational sex stereotypes. <u>Sex Roles, 8,</u> 301-308.

Krippendorff, K. (1980). <u>Content analysis: An introduction to methodology.</u> Newbury Park, CA: Sage.

Smith, C. P. (Ed.). (1992). <u>Motivation and personality: Handbook of thematic content analysis.</u> Cambridge: Cambridge University Press.

ethical conduct of the research. Broadly speaking, psychological researchers are expected to protect the dignity, privacy, and safety of their research participants and to do research that is technically sound and beneficial to society.

Here are some questions to guide you as you think about what to write in your proposal:

- ◆ What will the participants be asked to do?
- ◆ Can you think of any psychological or physical risks to the participants?
- ◆ Will any deception be used, and if so, why do you believe it to be necessary?
- ◆ How will the participants be debriefed (and "dehoaxed" if you are permitted to use a deception procedure)?
- ◆ How will the participants be recruited, and is this recruitment procedure noncoercive?
- ◆ How will the participants be told what the purpose of the study is and that they are free to withdraw at any time without penalty?
- ◆ How will the participants' informed consent be secured?
- ◆ What steps will be taken to ensure the confidentiality of the data?

Tempus Fugit

Because time flies when you are writing a required paper for a course, here are two final tips:

- ◆ Turn in your proposal on time. Instructors are also very busy people, and they (like you) schedule their work. Turning in a proposal late is like waving a red flag that signals the wrong message to your instructor. Instead of communicating that you are responsible and reliable and think clearly, this "red flag" signals that you may be none of the above.
- ◆ Be precise. In Lewis Carroll's *Through the Looking Glass,* Alice (of *Alice in Wonderland*) comes upon Humpty Dumpty, who uses a word in a way that Alice says she does not understand. He smiles contemptuously and says, "Of course you don't—till I tell you. . . . When *I* use a word, it means just what I choose it to mean—neither more nor less." Unlike Humpty Dumpty, you do not have the luxury of telling your instructor to "take it or leave it." Nor do you have the extra time to keep resubmitting the proposal because you did not make an effort to be precise.

Chapter Four

ORGANIZING THE ESSAY

*O*nce *you have completed your literature search and are ready to begin drafting your essay, the next step is to prepare a detailed outline. The imposition of form will help you collect and refine your thoughts as you shape the paper. If you did not outline before the fact, you should at least do so afterward. If a logical, ordered form does not emerge, the weak spots will become apparent and you can fix them. (If you are writing a research report, you can skip this chapter and go on to Chapter Five.)*

Where to Start

A weak structure or a lack of structure is a common flaw in students' essays. A weak structure is a sure sign that the student did not develop an outline before beginning to write—or even after drafting the paper. Without an outline, the essay can ramble on endlessly, and reading it becomes an exercise in shaking hands with an octopus. In contrast, if you have a good outline, you will find that the paper almost writes (or rewrites) itself. You know where your ideas and sentences are heading, and it is more likely that you will be able to adhere to the time schedule you have set yourself.

If done correctly, your outline will imply a logical progression of the points of interest that you want to cover. You will be able to produce a parallel construction of the text and a balanced hierarchy of organization. Initially, you can generate a tentative and general outline as you use the library's resources to search for reference material. Use comparison and contrast as a way of structuring the outline in your mind; then pull together facts or studies to document and expand on your subtopics.

Some students find it difficult to begin making an outline. If you are having a problem getting started, there are three tricks you can try:

◆ Think of the outline as a table of contents based on the headings you might want to use.

◆ Shop around for an interesting quote that encourages fresh thinking and can later launch the introduction as well as capture and focus the reader's interest.

◆ Ask yourself the reporter's questions: *who, what, when, where,* and *why.*

Before you begin writing (discussed in Chapter Six), you will probably want to revise the preliminary outline so that it reflects the organizational structure you will use to shape the paper. This structure should be viewed not as carved in stone, but as something plastic that you can mold to your ideas as they continue to develop. Use the structure to guide you, but do not be afraid to change it if your thinking changes.

Making Ideas Parallel

Outline items can be set down in topics, sentences, or paragraphs. The specific form you choose should be the only one used in the outline so that all the ideas are parallel. In the following outline fragment, based very loosely on Anne's paper in Appendix A, the ideas are clearly not parallel:

    I. What is intelligence? What does "g-centric" mean? What will follow?

   II. Two views

      A. Traditional—the general overriding factor of intelligence is measured by every task on an intelligence test

      B. Spearman's psychometric contribution

      C. Developmental psychologists, following Piaget, argue for general mental structures

      D. <u>The Bell Curve</u>

The problem with this abbreviated outline is that it is a hodgepodge of questions, topics, idea fragments, and a book title. Working with this jumble is like swimming upstream. Such an outline will only sabotage your efforts to put thoughts and notes into a logical sequence. Contrast this incoherent structure with the parallel structure of the following outline as it covers the section of Anne's essay called "Two Views of Intelligence":

    I. Two views of intelligence

      A. The traditional view

         1. General overriding trait (Spearman)

            a. "g-centric" notion of intelligence

            b. Jensen and heritability

         2. Piaget's idea of general structures of the mind

            a. Universal developmental sequence

            b. Biological operationalization (speed of neural transmission)

         3. Herrnstein and Murray's book on role of g in society

Putting Ideas in Order

Whether you use topics, sentences, or paragraphs for your outline, try to group your information in descending order, from the most general facts or ideas to the most specific details and examples. We see this approach clearly in the parallel format of the outline shown immediately above. The same rule applies whether you are outlining definitions and evaluation criteria or the nature of a specific theory that you plan to develop further in the first draft:

> II. Gardner's theory of "intelligences"
>> A. Definition of intelligence
>>> 1. Problem solving and creative abilities
>>> 2. Evaluation criteria
>>>> a. Isolation if brain-damaged
>>>> b. Existence of exceptional populations
>>>> c. Unique core operations
>>>> d. Distinctive developmental history
>>>> e. Existence of primitive antecedents
>>>> f. Openness to experimentation
>>>> g. Prediction of performance on tests
>>>> h. Information content accessible
>> B. Kinds of intelligence
>>> 1. Logical-mathematical
>>> 2. Linguistic
>>> 3. Spatial
>>> 4. Bodily-kinesthetic
>>> 5. Musical
>>> 6. Personal
>>>> a. Intrapersonal
>>>> b. Interpersonal

Another convention in making an outline, as illustrated in Exhibit 15, is that if there is a subtopic division, there should be at least two subtopics, never only one. Facts, ideas, and concepts are classified by the use of roman numerals I, II, III; capitals A, B, C; arabic numerals 1, 2, 3; small letters a, b, c; and finally numbers and letters in parentheses. Thus, if you list I, you should list II (and perhaps III and IV and so on); if A, then B; if 1, then 2.

The roman numerals indicate the outline's main ideas. Indented capital letters provide main divisions within each main idea. The letters and numbers that follow list the supporting details and examples. Note the indentation of each subtopic. Any category can be expanded to fit the number of supporting details or examples that you wish to cover in the paper. Any lapses in logic are bound to surface if you use this system of organization, so you can catch and correct them before proceeding.

EXHIBIT 15 Subdivision of the outline

I.
  A.
  B.
    1.
    2.
        a.
        b.
            (1)
            (2)
                (a)
                (b)
II.

For example, look at the following abbreviated outline; Item B is clearly a conspicuous lapse in logic:

II. Gardner's theory of "intelligences"
  A. His definition of intelligence
  B. How did the concept of g originate?
  C. Seven kinds of intelligence

Item B should be moved from this section of the outline to the one pertaining to the g-centric view of intelligence. Some items may require a return to the library to clarify a point or to supplement parts of the outline with additional reference material.

Template for Writing and Note Taking

The outline is not only a way to organize your thoughts but also to make it easier to start writing. If you use the phrase or sentence format, the paper will almost write itself. We see this clearly in the following outline fragment:

II. Gardner's theory of "intelligences"
  A. Definition of intelligence
    1. ". . . the ability to solve problems, or to create products that are valued within one or more cultural settings" (Gardner, 1983, p. x)
    2. Intellectual talent must satisfy eight criteria (Gardner, 1983)
        a. Possible identification of intelligences by damage to particular areas of the brain
        b. Existence of exceptional populations (savants), implying the distinctive existence of a special entity

Had our hypothetical outline used complete sentences, the paper would write itself:

II. Gardner's theory of "intelligences"
  A. Definition of intelligence
    1. Gardner (1983) conceives of intelligence as "the ability to solve problems, or to create products that are valued within one or more cultural settings" (p. x).
    2. Gardner (1983) argues that a talent must fit eight criteria to be considered "intelligence."
      a. There is potential to isolate the intelligence by brain damage.
      b. Exceptional populations (e.g., savants) provide evidence for distinct entities.

In Chapter Two, we alluded to one other helpful hint about using an outline. The outline's coding system makes it convenient to code the notes you take during your literature search in the library. If your notes refer to section "II.B.1" of your outline, then you would record this code on the card, photocopy, or computer printout. In this way, order is brought to your notes. If you are using cards, for example, you can spread them on a large table and sort through them according to the section from your notes and the outline, each component enhancing the other.

Keep in mind, however, that the outline is only a guide. Its form will probably change as you integrate your notes.

Outlining After the Fact

Some students write their papers over more than one semester (for example, a senior thesis) and may feel they cannot outline at the start because they do not know where the final research will go. When they do sit down to write, they tend to incorporate material from their earlier drafts, but they do not make an outline first. Still other students find the process of making an outline too exacting, preferring instead to sit at a word processor and let the stream of ideas flow spontaneously.

If either case describes you, then be sure to outline after the fact. To assure yourself that your work has an appealing, coherent form—what psychologists call a "good gestalt"—make a "table of contents" of your final draft, and then do a more detailed outline within the headings and subheadings. Ask yourself:

- Is the discussion focused, and do the ideas flow from or build on one another?
- Is there ample development of each idea?
- Are there supporting details for each main idea discussed?
- Are the ideas balanced?
- Is the writing to the point, or have I gone off on a tangent?

An experienced writer working with a familiar topic might be able to achieve success without a detailed outline. But for others, the lack of an outline often creates havoc and frustration, not to mention wasted time and effort. If you would like to practice on someone else's work, try outlining some section of Anne's paper. Ask yourself how well her discussion addresses the five preceding questions. If you find problems with the structure of her discussion, think of ways she could have avoided them or corrected them before submitting the final draft.

Chapter Five

PLANNING THE RESEARCH REPORT

The basic structure and form of research reports in psychology have evolved over many years. In this chapter, we describe this structure and form in the context of the sample reports in Appendixes B and C. One report is that of an experimental study, and the other, of an archival study. The literature review of both reports, as is usually the case in research reports, involves only a few key studies. Knowing about the expected structure and form of your report will enable you to organize your thoughts. (If you are writing an essay, you can skip this chapter and go on to Chapter Six.)

The Basic Structure

Research methods texts routinely cover data collection and data analysis, and we will assume that you are mastering the techniques they describe. What remains is to develop a research report that will explain in clear language (a) what you did, (b) why you did it, (c) what you found out, (d) what it means, and (e) what you concluded. Well-written reports imply a logical progression in thought, and by adhering to the structure described in this chapter, you can create this kind of order in your finished report.

Looking again at Bruce's report (Appendix B) and Peter's report (Appendix C), we see that both have eight parts:

Title page
Abstract
Introduction
Method
Results
Discussion
References
End material (tables, figures, appendixes)

Except for the layout of the title page and the addition of appendixes in Bruce's and Peter's reports, the basic structure corresponds to a standard reporting format that has evolved over many years in psychology. Later on, we will discuss the layout of the paper (for example, the "page header" in the upper-right corner). You can see that the title page in the two reports is straightforward, and therefore we can focus our attention on the remaining parts.

Abstract

Although the abstract appears at the beginning of your report, it is actually written after you complete the rest of your paper. The abstract provides a concise summary of your report. Think of it as a distillation of the important points covered in the body of the report. Thus, in succinct paragraphs in the sample research reports, Bruce and Peter summarize what they did, what they found, and what they concluded.

When planning your abstract, answer these questions as concisely as possible:

◆ What was the objective or purpose of my research study?
◆ What principal method did I use?
◆ Who were the research participants?
◆ What were my major findings?
◆ What did I conclude from these findings?

More detailed and more specific statements about methods, results, and conclusions are given in the body of your report. The brief summary of the abstract lets the reader anticipate what your report is about.

Introduction

The introduction provides the rationale for your research and prepares the reader for the methods you have chosen. Thus, you should give a concise history and background of your topic, leading into your hypotheses or questions. For example, Bruce cites data that underscore the importance of his topic and then summarizes the relevant results of previous research on the topic. In this way, he develops a logical foundation for his hypotheses. Peter's report also begins with some background data and shows an appealing logical order that leads us directly into his hypotheses.

Your literature review should show the development of your hypotheses or exploratory questions and the reason(s) you believe the research topic is worth studying. The strongest introductions are those that state the research problem or the hypotheses in such a way that the Method section appears to be a natural consequence of that statement. If you can get readers to think when they later see your Method section, "Yes, of course, that's what this researcher had to do to answer this question," then you will have succeeded in writing a strong introduction. Here are some questions to ask yourself as you plan the introduction:

- ◆ What was the purpose of my study?
- ◆ What terms need to be defined?
- ◆ How does my study build on or derive from other studies?
- ◆ What were my working hypotheses or expectations?

Method

The next step is to detail the methods and procedures used. If you used research participants, then you should describe them (for example, age, sex, and number of participants, as well as the way they were selected and any other details that will help to specify them.) Psychologists are trained to ask questions about the generalizability of research results. Your instructor will be thinking about the generalizability of your findings across both persons and settings (that is, the "external validity" of your results). For example, if your research participants were college students, then the instructor may ask whether your results can be generalized beyond this specialized population. (For an informative discussion of this issue, read D. O. Sears, "College Sophomores in the Laboratory: Influence of a Narrow Data Base on Social Psychology's View of Human Nature," *Journal of Personality and Social Psychology,* 1986, Vol. 51, pp. 515–530.)

Also included in this section should be a description of any tests or measures and the context in which they were used. Even if you used well-known, standardized tests (TAT, MMPI, or WAIS, for example), it is still a good idea to describe them in a few sentences. By describing them, you tell the instructor that you understand the nature and purpose of the instruments you used.

For example, suppose you used M. Snyder's Self-Monitoring Scale (see "Self Monitoring of Expressive Behavior," *Journal of Personality and Social Psychology,* 1974, Vol. 30, pp. 526–537). The instructor will expect you to have done a background search to learn more about this instrument and will suppose you have discovered that research has shown this test to consist of three different dimensions (see "An Analysis of the Self-Monitoring Scale," by S. R. Briggs, J. M. Cheek, and A. H. Buss, *Journal of Personality and Social Psychology,* 1980, Vol. 38, pp. 679–686). The question is how to put this information together in your report. In your report, you might say something like:

> Subjects were presented with Snyder's (1974) 25-item Self-Monitoring Scale, which was designed to measure the extent of self-observation and self-control guided by situational cues to social appropriateness. Briggs, Cheek, and Buss (1980) showed the multidimensional nature of this test, identifying three distinct factors that form internally consistent subscales. The Extraversion Subscale was described by Briggs et al. as tapping the respondent's chronic tendency to be the center of attention in groups, to tell stories and jokes, and so on. The Other-Directedness Subscale was described as measuring the respondent's willingness to change his or her behavior to suit others. The Acting Subscale was described as assessing liking and being good at speaking and entertaining.

However, suppose you need to report only the nature of a particular measure and not any follow-up inferences by other researchers. For example, assume you used the Need for Cognition Scale created by J. T. Cacioppo and R. E. Petty (see "The Need for Cognition," *Journal of Personality and Social Psychology,* 1982, Vol. 42, pp. 116–131). You can describe the measure as follows:

> Subjects were presented with Cacioppo and Petty's (1982) Need for Cognition Scale. This is an 18-item measure of the tendency to engage in and enjoy thinking.

If you know something about the reliability and validity of the measure you chose, include this information as well (along with the appropriate citation).

Results

In the next major section, describe your findings. You might plan to show the results in a table or figure, as in the sample reports. Do not make your instructor guess what you are thinking; label your table or figure fully, and discuss the data in the narrative of this section so that it is clear what they represent. It is not necessary to repeat the results from the table or figure in your narrative; simply tell what they mean.

Ask yourself the following questions as you structure your Results section:

- What did I find?
- How can I say what I found in a careful, detailed way?
- Is what I am planning to say precise and to the point?
- Will what I have said be clear to the reader?
- Have I left out anything of importance?

This section should consist of a careful, detailed analysis that strikes a balance between being discursive and being falsely or needlessly precise:

- You are guilty of *false precision* when something inherently vague is presented in overly precise terms. Suppose you used a standard attitude measure in your research, and suppose the research participants responded on a 5-point scale from "strongly agree" to "strongly disagree." It would be falsely precise to report the means to a high number of decimal places, because your psychological measure was not that sensitive to slight variations in attitudes.
- You are guilty of *needless precision* when (almost without thinking about it) you report something much more exactly than the circumstances require. For example, reporting the weight of mouse subjects to six decimal places might be within the bounds of your measuring instrument, but the situation does not call for such exactitude.

Incidentally, a common mistake in student papers (and even in journal articles by authors who should know better) is that when reporting attitudinal scores based on labeled 5-point scales, they are called "Likert scales." Technically, a *Likert scale* (named after Rensis Likert, its inventor) implies that the scale was developed by a particular method (called "summated ratings" by Likert). But this is not what most researchers really mean when they say they used a Likert scale. Some researchers skirt this problem by using the term "Likert-type scale," by which they merely mean that the response alternatives were accompanied by phrases or words (for example, "very favorable," "favorable," "neutral," "unfavorable," and "very unfavorable"), but they did not use the method of summated ratings to develop the scale. If this is all you mean, you can simply say something like "The response scale ranged from 'very favorable' (1) to 'very unfavorable' (5)."

Another convention that many students find confusing is the way that p values are to be presented. Many statisticians recommend reporting the actual descriptive level of significance because it carries more information than the phrases "significant difference" or "no significant difference at the 5% level." There is something absurd, they would argue, about regarding as a "real" effect one that is supported by $p = .05$ and as a "zero" effect one that is supported by $p = .06$. We recommend several options. One is to list a string of zeros such as "$p = .00000025$." Another option is to use scientific notation as a more compact way to show a very small p value. That is, instead of reporting $p = .00000025$, you report 2.5×10^{-7}, where -7 (i.e., the exponent of 10) tells us to count 7 places to the left of the decimal in 2.5 and make that the decimal place. In Peter's report (in Appendix C), the exponent is denoted by the letter E, which is also acceptable; thus we would report 2.5E-7. Of course, if you are looking up p values in a statistical table, you may not have the option of reporting them precisely. Thus, still another option is to state only that p is less than (<) or greater than (>) the particular column value in the statistical table, but do not confuse "nonsignificance" with "no effect." If there is zero effect, then the expected value of the t statistic equals 0, the F statistic equals approximately 1, and the chi-square (χ^2) statistic is equal to the degrees of freedom (df) of the χ^2.

Discussion

In the Discussion section, you will use the facts you have gathered to form a cohesive unit. A review of the introductory section is often helpful. Think about how you will discuss your research findings in light of your original hypotheses. Did serendipity (discussed in Chapter One) play a role in your study? If so, detail the unexpected by-products and ideas.

Try to write "defensively" without being too blatant about it. That is, be your own devil's advocate, and ask yourself what a skeptical reader might see as the other side of your argument or conclusion. In particular, look for shortcomings or critical inconsistencies, and anticipate the reader's reaction to them. If you cannot find any holes in your argument or conclusion, ask a clever friend to help you out by listening to your argument or conclusion.

Here are some additional questions to consider as you begin to structure this section:

- What was the purpose of my study?
- How do my results relate to that purpose?
- Were there any serendipitous findings of interest?
- How valid and generalizable are my findings?
- Are there larger implications in these findings?
- Is there an alternative way to interpret my results?

If you believe there are larger implications of your research findings, then the Discussion section is the place to spell them out. Are there implications for further research? If so, propose them here. In Appendix B, in his final paragraph, Bruce suggests ideas for future research. In Appendix C, Peter mentions the limitations of his sample and raises ideas for further research.

Incidentally, some researchers add a separate Conclusions section when they want to separate the ideas and arguments in the Discussion from some pithy conclusions. However, it is quite proper to treat the final paragraph of your Discussion section as the place for your conclusions. In either case, your conclusions should be stated as clearly and precisely as possible.

References

Once you have made plans for writing the body of the report, give some thought to your reference material again. You will need to include an alphabetized listing of all the sources of information you drew from, and it is essential that every citation be listed in your References section. To avoid retracing your steps in the library, keep a running list of the material that will appear in this section as you progress through the early preparation of your report. You can create a separate file called "References" and then copy and paste them into your paper's References section. If at the last minute you suddenly find you need to recheck the author, title, or publisher of a particular book, remember that you can go to http://lcweb.loc.gov/catalog to use the Library of Congress's on-line catalog.

End Material

The APA publication manual stipulates that tables and figures be placed in the manuscript after the References section, which is a convenience for the copyeditor and the printer. The papers in Appendixes B and C follow this style, as many instructors prefer that students use it. However, since your paper is not being submitted for publication, your instructor may permit you to insert tables and figures within the narrative section of your paper; this is easy enough to do if you are using a standard word-processing program. If you must have footnotes, the APA manual states that they belong on a separate page immediately after the References section and before any tables or figures, which is another convenience for the printer of journal articles. Not all instructors insist on this format, and you should check with your instructor if you have a question about how to proceed.

Many instructors recommend that the final section of the student's report be an appendix in which the raw materials and computations of the investigation are displayed. For example, if you used a lengthy test or questionnaire (which cannot be properly presented in the limited space of the Method section), then include it in the appendix. In Appendix C, notice that Peter includes his coding sheet for raters in his first appendix (labeled "A"). If your instructor would also like to see your calculations on the raw data, then they belong in an appendix (see Bruce's and Peter's reports). If you did the calculations by hand (as Bruce and Peter did), then it is proper simply to photocopy them.

Whether or not your instructor requires an appendix (or stipulates a different list of items to be included), it is very important that you keep all your notes and data until the instructor has returned your report and you have received a grade in the course—just in case the instructor has questions about your work.

Organizing Your Thoughts

In the preceding chapter, we described how to make an outline for the essay. The research report does not require a gross outline because its formal structure already provides a skeleton waiting to be fleshed out. Nevertheless, all researchers find it absolutely essential to organize their thoughts about each section before writing the first draft. There are three ways to do this:

♦ If you would like to learn about outlining, examine Chapter Four for guidelines on how to outline before or after the fact.
♦ You can make notes on separate index cards for each major point (for example, the rationale of the study, the derivation of each hypothesis, and each background study) and draw on these notes to write your first draft.
♦ You can simply make a computer file of such notes.

If you are still having a hard time getting going, here are two more tips:

♦ Imagine you are sitting across a table from a friend; tell your "friend" what you found.
♦ Take a tape recorder for a walk; tell it what you found in your research.

No matter what approach you favor, make sure that your notes or files are accurate and complete. If you are summarizing someone else's study, then you must note the full citation. If you are quoting someone, include the statement in quotation marks and make sure that you have copied it exactly.

Chapter Six

WRITING AND REVISING

*W*riting a first draft is a little like taking the first dip in chilly *ocean waters on a hot day. It may be uncomfortable at the outset but feels better once you get used to it. In this chapter, we provide some pointers to buoy you up as you begin writing. We also provide tips to help you revise your work.*

Sorting Through Your Material

Back in 1947, there was a fascinating story in newspapers and magazines about two brothers, the Collyers, who were found dead in a rubbish-filled mansion at Fifth Avenue and 128th Street in New York City. On receiving a tip that one brother, Homer Collyer, had died, the police forced their way into the mansion with crowbars and axes. They found all of the entrances to the house blocked by wrapped packages of newspapers, hundreds of cartons, and all kinds of junk (14 grand pianos, most of a Model-T Ford, the top of a horse-drawn carriage, a tree limb 7 feet long and 20 inches in diameter, an organ, a trombone, a cornet, three bugles and five violins, three World War I bayonets, and 10 clocks, including one 9 feet high and weighing 210 pounds). The rooms and hallways were honeycombed with tunnels through all this debris and booby-trapped so as to come crashing down on any intruder. The police began searching for the other brother, Langley, who had been caring for Homer, as it was thought that he might have phoned in with the tip. After 8 weeks of burrowing through the incredible mess, on April 8, 1947, they found the body of Langley Collyer wedged between a chest of drawers and a bedspring, killed by one of his own booby traps.

For students writing essays and research reports, the lesson of the Collyer brothers is that it is not always easy to discard things you have made an effort to save, including notes, studies, and quotes that you have gone to the trouble to track down. But quantity cannot replace quality and relevance in the material you save for your research report or essay. Instructors are more impressed by tightly reasoned papers than by ones that are overflowing with superfluous material. It is best to approach the writing and revising stage with an open but focused mind, that is, a mind that is focused on the objective but that is at the same time open to discarding irrelevant material (not research data, however).

The Self-Motivator Statement

To begin the first draft, write down somewhere for yourself the purpose or goal you have in mind (that is, what your paper will be about). Keep this "self-motivator statement" brief so that you have a succinct focus for your thoughts as you begin to set them down on paper or enter them into your word processor.

If we refer to the three papers, we can imagine the following self-motivators:

From Anne

My essay will contrast the traditional view of intelligence with Gardner's view, which illustrates what I call the multiplex approach, and I will tell how he has answered his critics.

From Bruce

I'm going to describe how I found that tipping increases when people are given a small gift, and how the manipulation of a reciprocity effect can further increase tipping.

From Peter

I found that children's books more often portray female characters as working in the household and male characters as working outside the home; I will cover the implications of these findings for the perpetuation of gender-based stereotypes.

This trick of using a self-motivator statement can help to concentrate your thoughts and make the task of writing seem less formidable. The self-motivator is a good way simply to get you going and keep you clearheaded, and it is also a good way to filter out material that can be discarded. You will be less apt to go off on a tangent if you remind yourself of exactly where you want your paper to go.

The Opening

A good opening is crucial if you want to engage the reader's attention and interest. Some writers are masters at creating good openings, but many technical articles and books in psychology start out ponderously. There are certainly enough cases of ponderous writing so that we need not give examples. But what about openings that grip our minds and make us want to delve further into the work?

One way to begin your paper in an inviting way is to pose a stimulating question. For example, Sissela Bok opened her book *Lying: Moral Choice in Public and Private Life* (Pantheon, 1978) with a number of questions:

> Should physicians lie to dying patients so as to delay the fear and anxiety which the truth might bring them? Should professors exaggerate the excellence of their students on recommendations in order to give them a better chance in a tight job market? Should parents conceal from children the fact that they were adopted? Should social scientists send investigators masquerading as patients to physicians in order to learn about racial and sexual biases in diagnosis and treatment? Should government lawyers lie to Congressmen who might otherwise oppose a much-needed welfare bill? And should journalists lie to those from whom they seek information in order to expose corruption? (p. xv)

Does this opening make you want to read further?

Another technique is to impress on readers the paradoxical nature of a timely issue. In *Obedience to Authority* (Harper, 1969), Stanley Milgram began as follows:

> Obedience is as basic an element in the structure of social life as one can point to. Some system of authority is a requirement of all communal living, and it is only the man dwelling in isolation who is not forced to respond, through defiance or submission, to the commands of others. Obedience, as a determinant of behavior, is of particular relevance to our time. It has been reliably established that from 1933 to 1945 millions of innocent people were systematically slaughtered on command. Gas chambers were built, death camps were guarded, daily quotas of corpses were produced with the same efficiency as the manufacture of appliances. These inhumane policies may have originated in the mind of a single person, but they could only have been carried out on a massive scale if a very large number of people obeyed orders. (p. 1)

The passage above was written before there were concerns about sexist language: Milgram's use of the word *man* ("it is only the man dwelling in isolation") as a general term for men and women is now considered improper usage. Instead, he could have said "people dwelling in isolation" (we return to this issue later). However, perhaps you are thinking, "What does Milgram's or Bok's work have to do with me? These are Ph.D. psychologists who were writing for publication, but I'm just writing a paper for a course." The answer any instructor will give you is that an expectation of good writing that captures the reader's attention and draws the reader into the message is not limited to published work (for example, it also applies to business correspondence, company memos, and applications for jobs).

What makes the opening paragraph of each of the three sample papers in the appendixes inviting? Each strikes a resonant chord in the reader. There are many other useful opening techniques: A definition, an anecdote (for example, the strange case of the Collyer brothers), a metaphor that compares or contrasts (such as using *the Collyer brothers* as a synonym for "pack rats"), an opening quotation (called an *epigraph*), and so on—all of these are devices that a writer can use to shape a beginning paragraph. Not only should the opening draw the reader into the work, but it should also serve to provide momentum for the writer as her or his words and ideas begin to flow. Anne begins her paper by implying a paradox, which is that we ordinarily speak of "intelligence" in many different ways, but psychologists have traditionally viewed it in one general way. Bruce and Peter start with some interesting facts, which immediately draw us into the logic of their introductions.

Settling Down to Write

Should you find yourself still having trouble beginning the introductory paragraph, try the trick of not starting at the opening of your paper. Start writing whatever section you feel will be the easiest, and then tackle the rest as your ideas begin to flow. When faced with the blank page or blank computer screen and flashing cursor, some students escape by taking a nap, watching MTV, or surfing the Net. Recognize these counterproductive moves for what they are, because they can drain your energies. Use them instead as rewards *after* you have done a good job of writing.

The following are general pointers to ensure that your writing will go as smoothly as possible:

- ◆ While writing, try to work in a quiet, well-lighted place in 2-hour stretches (dim lighting makes people sleepy).
- ◆ Go for a walk by yourself to collect your thoughts and to think of a sentence to get you going again (the fresh air will also be invigorating).
- ◆ If you are writing your first draft on a notepad, skip a line for each line you write down so you will have room for legible revisions. If you are using a word processor (which is a lot easier than using a notepad), set the Format menu to double-space (your final paper must be double-spaced anyway).
- ◆ Be sure to number the pages you write: It is maddening to mix up un-numbered pages. Better still, insert a numbered header so the pages will automatically appear as shown in the sample papers in the appendixes.
- ◆ When you take a break, try to stop at a point that is midway through an idea or a paragraph. In this way, you can resume work where you left off and avoid feeling stuck or having to start cold. You might also add a phrase or some notes that will get you back on the track once you return to your writing.
- ◆ Try to pace your work with time to spare so that you can complete the first draft and let it rest for 24 hours. When you return to the completed first draft after a night's sleep, your critical powers will be enhanced, and you will have a fresh approach to shaping the final draft.

Ethics of Writing and Reporting

The most fundamental ethical principle in psychological science is honesty in all aspects of the research, from its implementation to the final report of the procedures used, the results, and their implications. Examples of deliberate dishonesty are the falsification of data and the fabrication of results, which constitute fraud. In the same way that the professional career of a researcher who falsifies data or fabricates results is compromised, the consequences for the student writing a research report in which the data or results are fabricated may be harsh. This does not mean that "mock" (or hypothetical) data provided by the instructor constitute a breach of ethics; only representing as real data that are not real is dishonest.

Honesty in research reporting and other scholarly writing also means giving credit where it is due. For students, this means that if someone helped you or gave you an idea, you acknowledge that contribution in your narrative or in a footnote. For example, Peter mentions in his Method section that the instructor helped him with a sophisticated sampling method to pare down the pictorial material. Should your research later become part of an article authored by your instructor, the decision about whether you will be listed as a coauthor or mentioned in a footnote acknowledgment will depend on the nature of your contribution to the research. Analyzing data that the instructor provided may be a minor contribution deserving just a footnote acknowledgment, but if the article is substantially based on your individual efforts (as in a dissertation or thesis), you will usually be listed as a coauthor, possibly even as the principal author on a multiple-authored piece (depending on the circumstances of the multiauthor collaboration).

Another important ethical standard concerns the sharing of data with those who want to verify published claims by reanalyzing results. As specified in the APA publication manual, provided that it is possible to protect the confidentiality of the participants, and unless legal rights preclude the release of the data, psychologists are expected to make their results available to other competent professionals. Instructors have the option to require students writing research reports to provide the raw data on which the work is based. If confidentiality is a potential problem, the instructor will advise you on how the data should be coded to protect the privacy of those who have participated in your study.

Before we turn to what many instructors consider the most significant concern in student papers—the avoidance of plagiarism—we will mention one further standard with implications for students. The APA manual also cautions researchers not to publish, as original data, results that have already been published, unless there is an accompanying statement acknowledging that the data have been previously published. The implication for students writing papers is that it is wrong to submit the same work for additional credit in different courses. Possibly, it would be acceptable to base the literature review in a research report for one course on the more extensive review in a term paper for another course, but only with the full knowledge and consent of both instructors.

Avoiding Plagiarism

Perhaps the most nagging concern of most instructors who teach writing-intensive courses is conveying the meaning and consequences of plagiarism. The term *plagiarism,* which comes from the Latin word meaning "kidnapper," refers to theft of another person's ideas or work and passing it off as your own. It is crucial that you understand what constitutes plagiarism, as the penalties can be quite severe. Claiming not to know what constitutes plagiarism or lifting a passage (without putting it in quotes) because it was not easy to think of a way to express a thought or concept in one's own words is not an acceptable defense. Even if the plagiarism is "accidental," it is important to understand that stealing someone else's work is wrong and that, even if it is unintentional, the penalty in a class assignment or a thesis may be severe.

To illustrate how easy it is to avoid committing plagiarism, assume that a student doing a literature review came across Bok's *Lying: Moral Choice in Public and Private Life* (Pantheon, 1978) and copied down the following passage for future reference:

> Deceit and violence—these are two forms of deliberate assault on human beings. Both can coerce people into acting against their will. Most harm that can befall victims through violence can come to them also through deceit. But deceit controls more subtly, for it works on belief as well as action. Even Othello, whom few would have dared to try to subdue by force, could be brought to destroy himself and Desdemona through falsehood. (p. 18)

There is no problem so far. The student has copied the passage accurately and has noted the page on which it appeared. The problem arises when the student decides to use this passage and simply change a word or two to make it sound a little different. No need to mention Bok's book, he thinks, because no one will bother to check, and even if the instructor should happen to recognize this passage, why, the student can say that he simply "forgot" to give the author of that material full credit. The student submits an essay containing the following passage:

> Deceit and violence are two forms of deliberate assault on human beings. Both can coerce people into acting against their will. Most harm that can happen to people through violence can also happen to them through deceit. However, deceit controls more subtly, because it works on belief as well as action. Even Othello, whom few would have dared to try to subdue by force, could be brought to destroy himself and Desdemona through falsehood.

Although it might sound like an A paper, the passage when seen in the context of the rest of the paper may stick out like a sore thumb, and instructors are sensitive to inconsistencies like these. If the student is caught, he will receive an F in the course. Even if not caught red-handed, he must nevertheless live with the knowledge of his deceit and worry that his dishonesty may come back to haunt him.

How might the student have used this work without falling into plagiarism? The answer is simply to put quotes around the material he wants to copy verbatim—and then give a complete citation. Even if he just wanted to paraphrase the work, he is still responsible for giving full credit to the original author. Here is a reasonable paraphrase:

> Bok (1978) makes the case that deceit and violence "both can coerce people into acting against their will" (p. 18). Deceit, she notes, controls more subtly because it affects belief. Using a literary analogy, she observes, "Even Othello, whom few would have dared to try to subdue by force, could be brought to destroy himself and Desdemona through falsehood" (p. 18).

If you find something on the World Wide Web you want to use, the same considerations of honesty apply. Some instructors have told us how they randomly check students' titles and phraseology using a search engine to look for stolen material or uncredited citations. One instructor told us how he typed the title of a student's paper into a search engine and the entire paper came up on a Web site! Electronic plagiarizing is no more acceptable than plagiarizing from printed matter.

Lazy Writing

On hearing that quotations and citations are not construed by definition as plagiarism, some lazy students submit papers saturated with quoted material. Unless you feel it absolutely essential, avoid quoting long passages throughout a paper. It may be necessary to quote or paraphrase some material (with a citation, of course), but your written work is expected to result from your own individual effort. Quoting a simple sentence that can easily be paraphrased signals lazy writing.

In other words, your paper should reflect *your* thoughts on a particular topic after you have carefully examined and synthesized material from the sources you feel are pertinent. The penalty for lazy writing is not as severe as that for plagiarism, although often it means a reduced grade. Avoid both problems: plagiarism and lazy writing. As noted earlier, it is a good idea to keep your notes, outlines, and rough drafts; one reason is that instructors will ask students for such material if a question arises about the originality of their work.

And finally, many students use terms that they do not understand, especially when dealing with technical material. Misuse of terms is also considered lazy writing (and bad scholarship as well). Always try to make your point in your own words. If someone else has said it much better than you can ever hope to say it, quote (and cite) or paraphrase (and cite) the other source. On the other hand, if you really cannot say it in your own words, then you do not understand it well enough to write about it.

Tone

As you write, there are certain basic style points to keep in mind. The *tone* of your paper refers to the manner in which you express your ideas to the reader. Your writing should not be dull; presumably you are writing on a topic that you find fascinating, inasmuch as you chose it.

Here are some hints on how to create the right tone:

- ◆ Strive for an explicit, straightforward, interesting but not emotional way of expressing your thoughts, findings, and conclusions.
- ◆ Avoid having your essay or research report read like a letter to a favorite aunt ("Here's what Jones and Smith say . . ." or "So I told the research participants . . .").
- ◆ Do not try to duplicate a reporter's slick style, familiar in the glib spoken reports on network TV and in supermarket tabloids.
- ◆ If your instructor finds it acceptable, it is certainly all right to use the first person ("I shall discuss . . ." or "My conclusion is that . . ."). But do not refer to yourself as *we* unless you are clearly referring to a collaborative effort with someone else.
- ◆ Strive for an objective, direct tone that keeps your reader subordinate to the material you are presenting. Do not write, "The reader will note that the results were . . ." Instead, write, "The results were . . ."
- ◆ A famous writing manual is *The Elements of Style* (Prentice Hall, 1979) by W. Strunk, Jr., and E. B. White. One of Professor Strunk's admonitions is "Omit needless words. Omit needless words. Omit needless words."

Nonsexist Language

The question of *word gender* has become a matter of some sensitivity among many writers, particularly in psychology. One reason to discourage sex bias in written and spoken communication is that words can influence people's thoughts and deeds, and we do not want to reinforce stereotypes or prejudiced behaviors. To be sure, there is sometimes a good reason not to use gender-free pronouns. Suppose a new drug has been tested only on male participants. If the researchers used only gender-free pronouns when referring to their participants, a reader might mistakenly infer that the results apply to both sexes.

The point, of course, is to think before you write. In her book *The Elements of Nonsexist Usage* (Prentice Hall, 1990), Val Dumond made the following observation concerning overuse of the word *man:* "When the word is used, that is the mental picture that is formed. The picture is what simultaneously represents a conceptual meaning to the interpreter. Since a female picture does not come to mind when the word *man* is used, it would follow that *man* does not represent in any way a female human" (p. 1).

When the issues of nonsexist language first gained prominence in psychology, researchers and others often used contrived words such as *s/he* and *he/she* to avoid sexist language. Experienced writers and editors have proposed various ways to circumvent the awkwardness of such forms and also the possible trap of gender-biased language. In general, beware of masculine nouns and pronouns that will give a sex bias to your writing. There are two simple rules:

◆ Use plural pronouns when you are referring to both genders, for instance, "They did . . ." instead of "He did . . ."; and ". . . to them" instead of ". . . to him."

◆ Use masculine and feminine pronouns if the situation calls for them. For example, if the study you are discussing used only male research participants, then the masculine pronouns are accurate. The forms *he/she* and *s/he* are not only awkward but in this case would mislead the reader into thinking that the research participants were both women and men.

Voice

The verb forms you use in your writing can speak with one of two voices: active or passive. You write in the *active voice* when you represent the subject of your sentence as performing the action expressed by your verb ("The research participant responded by . . ."). You write in the *passive voice* when the subject of your sentence undergoes the action expressed by your verb ("The response made by the research participant was . . .").

If you try to rely mainly on the active voice, you will have a more vital, compelling style:

Active Voice (Good)

In a classic book in psychology, Dollard and Miller (1950) hypothesized that frustration leads to aggression.

Passive Voice (Not as Good)

In a classic book on psychology, it was hypothesized by Dollard and Miller (1950) that frustration leads to aggression.

Verb Tense

The verb tenses you use in your paper can get into a tangle unless you observe the following basic rules:

◆ Use the *past tense* to report studies that were done in the past ("Jones and Smith found . . ."). If you are writing a research report, both Method and Results sections can usually be written in the past tense because your study has already been accomplished ("In this study, data *were* collected . . ." and "In these questionnaire answers, there *were* . . .").

◆ Use the *present tense* to define terms ("Multiplex, in this context, *refers* to . . ." and "A stereotype *is* defined as . . ."). The present tense is also frequently used to state a general hypothesis or to make a general claim ("Winter days *are* shorter than summer days.").

◆ The *future tense* can be saved for the section of your paper in which you discuss implications for further investigation ("Future research *will be* necessary . . ."), but it is not essential to use the future tense. You could say, "Further investigation *is* warranted."

Agreement of Subject and Verb

Make sure each sentence expresses a complete thought and has a *subject* (in general terms, something that performs the action) and a *verb* (an action that is performed or a state of being).

Subject and Verb Agree

The participants [subject] were [verb] students.

Because the subject is plural *(participants)* the verb form used *(were)* is also plural. This means the verb and subject agree, a basic rule of grammar.

In most sentence forms, achieving this agreement is a simple matter. But trouble can sometimes arise, so here are some tips:

◆ When you use *collective nouns* (those that name a group), they can be either singular or plural, for example, *committee, team,* and *faculty.* When you think of the group as a single unit, use a singular verb ("The union *is* ready to settle"). Plurals are called for when you want to refer to the components of a group ("The faculty *were* divided on the issue").

◆ Trouble can pop up when words come between subject and verb: "Therapy *[singular subject],* in combination with behavioral organic methods of weight gain, exemplifies *[singular verb form]* this approach." It would be incorrect to write, "Therapy, in combination with behavioral organic methods of weight gain, *exemplify [plural verb form]* this approach.

◆ Use a *singular verb form* after the following: *each, either, everyone, someone, neither, nobody.* Here is a correct usage: "When everyone is ready, the experiment will begin.

Common Usage Errors

Instructors see frequent usage errors in student papers. The inside front cover of this manual lists pairs of words that are both pronounced similarly *(homonyms)* and often confused with one another, such as *accept* ("receive") and *except* ("other than").

Another pair of confusing homonyms is *affect* and *effect*. In their most common form, the words *effect,* a noun meaning "outcome" (as in "Aggression is often an *effect* of frustration"), and *affect,* a verb meaning "to influence" (as in "Frustration *affects* how a person behaves"), are frequently confused. Moreover, *effect* can also be a verb meaning "to bring about" (as in "The procedure *effected* a measurable improvement"), and in psychology, *affect* can be a noun meaning "emotion" (as in "Subjects may show a positive *affect*").

Another potential source of problems is the incorrect use of the singular and plural of some familiar terms, for instance:

Singular	*Plural*
analysis	analyses
anomaly	anomalies
appendix	appendixes or appendices (both are correct)
criterion	criteria
datum	data
hypothesis	hypotheses
phenomenon	phenomena
stimulus	stimuli

For example, one common usage error is the confusion of *phenomena (plural term)* with *phenomenon (singular term)*. It would be incorrect to write "This *[singular pronoun]* phenomena *[plural subject]* is *[singular verb]* of interest." The correct form is either "This phenomenon is . . ." or "These phenomena are . . ."

Although you will find that words like *data* and *media* are often construed as singular, the general rule is that until there is no question about something's being correct, it is good to be on the safe side (so as not to be criticized by sticklers). In this case, the safe side is to interpret *data* and *media* as plural words. Thus, it would be unsafe to write "The data *[plural subject]* indicates *[singular verb]* . . ." or "The data shows . . ." To be on the safe side, you would write "The data indicate . . ." or "The data show . . ."

One common source of confusion is in the misuse of the words *between* and *among*. As a general rule, use *between* when you are referring to two items only; use *among* when there are more than two items. For example, it would be incorrect to write "between the three of them."

There is, however, one anomaly that you can do nothing about correcting. In the analysis of variance (abbreviated ANOVA), conventional usage says "between sum of squares" and the "between mean square," even if the number of conditions being compared is more than two.

Other common problems concern the use of some *prefixes* in psychological terms:

- The prefix *inter-* means "between" (for example, *interpersonal* means "between persons"); the prefix *intra-* means "within" (for example, *intrapersonal* means "within the person").
- The prefix *intro-* means "inward" or "within"; the prefix *extra-* means "outside" or "beyond." The psychological term *introverted* thus refers to an "inner-directed personality"; the term *extraverted* indicates an "outer-directed personality."
- The prefix *hyper-* means "too much"; the prefix *hypo-* means "too little." Hence, the term *hypothyroidism* refers to a deficiency of thyroid hormone, whereas *hyperthyroidism* denotes an excess of thyroid hormone, and a *hyperactive* child is one who is excessively active.

Although not strictly a usage error, referring to those who participated in the research as "subjects" is no longer recommended by the APA. Because the term *subjects* is seen as passive and nondescriptive, the recommendation is to be more specific by using terms such as *participants, respondents, children, patients,* and *clients.*

Numerals

Another source of bafflement can be the proper use of numerals in the APA style. In general, the APA recommends spelling out single-digit numbers and using numerals for numbers with more than one digit (both cardinal and ordinal). Among the exceptions to this rule are units of age and time (e.g., 4-year-old, 3 months, 2 days, 9 minutes) and numbers used in reference lists (e.g., pp. 4–6, 2nd ed., Vol. 4). Notice, for example, in Anne's discussion of the multiplex view, that she refers to "1 of 11 coauthors" because *one* is part of a group that includes a number above nine.

Punctuation

The correct use of the various punctuation marks will help prevent confusion in your writing. A *period* ends a declarative sentence. It also follows an abbreviation, as in the following common abbreviations of Latin words:

cf.	from *confer* ("compare")
e.g.	from *exempli gratia* ("for example")
et al.	from *et alia* ("and others")
et seq.	from *et sequens* ("and following")
ibid.	from *ibidem* ("in the same place")
i.e.	from *id est* ("that is")
op. cit.	from *opere citato* ("in the work cited")
viz.	from *videlicet* ("namely")

If you continually write *eg.* or *et. al.* in your paper, you will be telling the instructor, "I don't know the meaning of these terms!" The reason, of course, is that *e.g.* is the abbreviation of two words, not one; *eg.* announces that you believe (mistakenly) it is the abbreviation of one word. Putting a period after *et* tells the instructor that you believe (again, mistakenly) it is an abbreviation, which it is not; it is an entire Latin word.

Incidentally, the APA publication manual requires that abbreviations like *i.e.* and *e.g.* be used only in parentheses and tabular material, and that these abbreviations otherwise be spelled out:

Abbreviation ("e.g.") in Parentheses

Herrnstein and Murray's (1994) book was widely debated (e.g., Andery & Serio, 1997; Andrews & Nelkin, 1996; Carroll, 1997).

Spelled Out ("for example") When Not in Parentheses

Herrnstein and Murray's (1994) book was widely debated; see, for example, work by Andery and Serio (1997), Andrews and Nelkin (1996), and Carroll (1997).

On the subject of abbreviations, some others that you may encounter are the short forms of English words:

anon.	for *anonymous*
ch.	for *chapter*
diagr.	for *diagram*
ed.	for *editor* or *edition*
fig.	for *figure*
ms.	for *manuscript*
p.	for *page*
pp.	for *pages*
rev.	for *revised*
vol.	for *volume*

The various uses of the *comma* include the following:

♦ Use commas to separate three or more items in a series ("Smith, Jones, and Brown" or "high, medium, and low scorers").
♦ Use commas to set off introductory phrases in a sentence ("In another experiment performed 10 years later, the same researchers found . . .").
♦ Use commas to set off thoughts or phrases that are incidental to or that qualify the basic idea of the sentence ("This variable, although not part of the researchers' main hypothesis, was also examined").
♦ Put a comma before connecting words *(and, but, or, nor, yet)* when they join independent clauses ("The participant lost weight, but he was still able to . . .").

The *semicolon* (;) is used to join independent clauses in a sentence when connecting words are omitted. A semicolon is called for when the thoughts in the two independent clauses are close, and the writer wishes to emphasize this point or to contrast the two thoughts:

Semicolon for Connecting Thoughts

Anorexia nervosa is a disorder in which the victims literally starve themselves; despite their emaciated appearance, they consider themselves overweight.

In most instances, these long sentences can be divided into shorter ones, which will be clearer:

No Semicolon

Anorexia nervosa is a disorder in which the victims literally starve themselves. Despite their emaciated appearance, they consider themselves overweight.

Use a *colon* (:) to indicate that a list will follow, or to introduce an amplification. The colon tells the reader, "Note what follows":

Colon to Indicate That a List Follows:

Participants were given the following items: (a) four calling birds, (b) three French hens, (c) two turtle doves . . .

Colon to Introduce an Amplification

Examples of the amplification use of the colon are the titles of Anne's, Bruce's, and Peter's papers. Another example of amplification would be:

Gardner (1983) postulated two forms of the personal intelligences: interpersonal and intrapersonal intelligence.

Quotations

Double quotation marks (". . .") are used to enclose direct quotations in the narrative of the paper, and *single quotation marks* ('. . .') indicate a quote within a quote:

Quotation Marks

Participant B responded, "My feeling about this difficult situation was summed up in a nutshell by Jim when he said, 'It's a tough job, but somebody has to do it.'"

Here are more rules about punctuation when using quotations in your paper:

◆ If the appropriate punctuation is a comma or a period, it is included *within* the quotation marks.

- Colons and semicolons always come *after* the closing quotation marks.
- When the quotation is 40 or more words, it is set off from the body of the prose by means of indented margins, and quotation marks around the quoted passage are omitted.

Passage Containing Lengthy Quotation and Internal Quotation

What practical implications did Rosenthal and Jacobson (1968) draw from their research findings? They wrote:

> As teacher-training institutions begin to teach the possibility that teachers' expectations of their pupils' performance may serve as self-fulfilling prophecies, there may be a new expectancy created. The new expectancy may be that children can learn more than had been believed possible, an expectation held by many educational theorists, though for quite different reasons. . . . The new expectancy, at the very least, will make it more difficult when they encounter the educationally disadvantaged for teachers to think, "Well, after all, what can you expect?" The man on the street may be permitted his opinions and prophecies of the unkempt children loitering in a dreary schoolyard. The teacher in the schoolroom may need to learn that those same prophecies within her may be fulfilled; she is no casual passerby. Perhaps Pygmalion in the classroom is more her role. (pp. 181–182)

Notice that the quotation begins, "As teacher-training institutions" and ends "in the classroom is more her role"; the page numbers on which the passage appears in Rosenthal and Jacobson's book are shown in parentheses at the end.

This passage (like that by Milgram, quoted previously) was written before there were concerns about the question of assigning gender, and Rosenthal and Jacobson referred to the teacher as "she" and to "the man on the street." If you wanted to make the point that the quoted passage ignores gender, then you might insert in brackets the underlined word *sic* (Latin, meaning "thus," indicating that a word or phrase that appears strange or incorrect is quoted verbatim). The two quoted sentences would then look like this:

> The man [sic] on the street may be permitted his opinions and prophecies of the unkempt children loitering in a dreary schoolyard. The teacher in the schoolroom may need to learn that those same prophecies within her [sic] may be fulfilled; she is no casual passer-by.

Note that we did not insert *sic* after every gender term in the quoted passage. In the first sentence, the masculine pronoun *his* was not set off by *sic* because the reference is "man on the street." In the second sentence, the feminine pronoun *she* is also not set off, because the referent is "within her."

Revising

In the next chapter, we consider the details of producing your final draft. Revising the first draft of your paper is best done after you have been able to leave the material entirely. When you approach your writing after having taken such a break (ideally, 24 hours or more), your critical powers will be sharper. Syntax errors, lapses in logic, and other problems will become evident, so that smoothing out these sections will be a relatively simple chore.

As you reread and polish your writing, consider the following dos and don'ts:

- Be concise.
- Break up long paragraphs that contain a lot of disparate ideas into smaller, more coherent paragraphs.
- Be specific.
- Choose words for what they mean, not just for how they sound.
- Double-check punctuation.
- Don't use a long word when a short word will do.
- Don't be redundant (for example, "most unique" is redundant).
- Don't let spelling errors mar your writing.
- If you are unsure about how to spell or use a word, or about whether particular words need to be hyphenated, check your dictionary.

If you are new to word processing (or are learning a new word-processing program), be sure you know how to save and back up your work when you are ready to start composing and revising. A good system will do this for you automatically at regular intervals, but you must specify the interval you want. It is a good idea to save and back up at least every hour. If there is a SAVE button on your screen, it is easy enough to click on it every once in a while. You never know when the electricity will suddenly go out or someone will playfully or accidentally hit a wrong key, sending your work into oblivion. Making a "backup" means not only storing something inside the computer's hard drive (that is, if it's *your* PC) but also copying it onto a disk. Our habit is also to make a printout at the end of the day. Having a printed copy will allow you to inspect and modify the layout to make sure it looks the way you want it to. It also allows you to polish your writing in a format that is tangible. Sometimes spelling errors and murky passages that are less apparent on-screen jump out as your eye traverses a printed page.

Chapter Seven

PRODUCING THE FINAL DRAFT

This chapter provides you with general guidelines and tips for producing a finished product. The layout and production of your final draft are like the icing on a cake. If the underlying structure is sound, the result will be smooth and predictable.

General Pointers

Working with a word processor means that the steps involved in first drafts, revisions, and final drafts are telescoped. These stages lose their formal definition because the computer allows you, with the stroke of a key or the click of a mouse, to shift or change words, sentences, paragraphs, and even entire sections as you compose and revise. In the old days, when students could use only a typewriter, it was painfully difficult to revise, because they had to equip themselves with scissors and glue to literally cut and paste and each time had to retype the paper. Notes, long quotations, references, tables, and figures that you will need for your final draft can be stored in your computer's memory or on a disk and retrieved as needed. You simply highlight the material you want to use, click on the COPY button (or the CUT button, if you really want to remove the material from one place and transfer it to another), insert the cursor in the place where you want to paste, and click on the PASTE button. The computer is not a substitute for the hard work of organizing your ideas, thinking them through, and expressing them clearly, but it releases you from an enormous amount of drudgery.

Good word-processing systems also have "spell check" and "grammar check" programs to catch mistakes and prompt you to correct them. However, these programs are not infallible, so do not let them lull you into a false sense of security. Your spell check is based on a dictionary (actually a word inventory) in the word-processing system, but many technical terms that psychologists and other professionals use may not be present in your word-processing inventory. If your spell check highlights a term that you know is spelled correctly, simply add it to the inventory. If any of the terms that appear inside the front and back covers of this manual are missing, start by adding them. You will discover useful technical terms as you go about your literature search; keep a list, and enter them into your inventory when you have a free moment. As many experienced writers know, grammar-check programs can be maddening, particularly when they "catch" acceptable stylistic variations and fail to recognize stylistic requirements that may have been violated. Although it is essential to keep the spell-check program active (and current), many experienced writers turn off the grammar check and depend on their own eyes and experience to catch mistakes and correct them.

Here are more general pointers as you set about producing the final product:

- Make sure the type is legible. If it is faint, invest in a new cartridge.
- Use double line spacing, and print on only one side of the paper, numbering pages in the upper-right corner as the sample papers illustrate.
- Make a second copy of the finished paper. The original is for your instructor, and the duplicate copy will ensure the immediate availability of an exact spare copy in case of an unforeseen problem.
- Let the right margin remain ragged (uneven). That is, do not use a justified right margin, which creates a block effect and, sometimes, odd spacing within lines.
- Set your font size to 11 or 12, and use a font like Times New Roman or Arial (that is, use a font that is easy to read).
- The APA recommended style for manuscripts submitted for publication is to use one space following all punctuation, but APA does not return manuscripts on the basis of the spacing around punctuation. Therefore, if you are in the habit of inserting two spaces after a period (which we are), do what is comfortable.

We turn now to other specifics of layout and processing that will help to give your finished product an inviting appearance.

Title Page Format

Glance at the title pages of the sample papers. The title summarizes the main idea of the project and is centered on the page. (Notice that the title appears again on page 3 of each sample paper.) A good title is succinct and yet adequately describes to the reader the gist of the work. You will already have arrived at a working title when you narrowed your topic and drafted a proposal (Chapter Three). That title can now be changed or made more specific if you feel it is no longer accurate or completely descriptive of the finished product. (Incidentally, the APA style is to capitalize prepositions of four or more letters in titles and headings, so you would capitalize "With," for example, if it appeared in the title of your paper.)

Other information is also shown on the title page of these sample papers:

The student's name (called the *byline*)
The number and name of the course or sequence for which the paper was
 written
The date the paper will be submitted

It is optional to show the instructor's name (if the paper is submitted for a course) or the adviser's name (if the paper is submitted to fulfill some other requirement, such as a "prelim" paper). If the paper is a thesis, you should include an acknowledgment page (after the title page) on which you thank your adviser and any others who extended a helping hand as you worked on your project. Incidentally, theses also usually include a table of contents page.

Notice that the page number in the upper-right corner is accompanied (on every page) by one or more words. These words are called *page headers,* and their purpose is to make it easy for the reader to identify each manuscript page if pages become separated. It is easy enough to insert a page header with most word-processing programs. In Microsoft Word, for example, you would click once on VIEW, then on HEADER AND FOOTER to bring up this menu; type in the key words, hit the space bar three times, and click on the button on the left (INSERT PAGE NUMBER). Click on the ALIGN RIGHT button in the toolbar on the Word screen display (which moves the header flush right), and close the HEADER AND FOOTER menu.

Some instructors insist that student papers for courses use title pages identical to those on manuscripts submitted to journals. Exhibit 16 recasts the title page of Bruce's research paper in this form. The "running head" is an abbreviated title that is printed at the top of the pages of a published article in some journals. The APA rule is that running heads cannot exceed 50 characters, counting letters, punctuation, and spaces between words. On the title page, the running head is placed at the left margin (flush left) and is typed in capital letters. The title of Bruce's required paper in Appendix B would be far too wordy for a journal submission, and Exhibit 16 shows how it might be shortened. The byline and affiliation are centered beneath the title of the paper. Incidentally, although it is not shown in Exhibit 16, many writers when submitting manuscripts to journals also include on the cover page their address for editorial correspondence, phone number, fax number, and E-mail address.

Headings

It is customary to break up the text of a manuscript with headings. You can derive these from the outline of your essay or, in the case of the research report, use the headings that are inherent in the structure of the report. Note, for example, how Anne's headings and subheadings lend symmetry to her paper, showing its progressive development in concise phrases. Her paper uses two formats of headings: center and flush left. The *center heading* is used to separate the paper into major sections, is written in uppercase and lowercase letters, and is not underlined. To subdivide the major sections, she

EXHIBIT 16 *Cover page of Bruce's paper in APA format*

Tipping Behavior   1

Running head: RESTAURANT TIPPING

Effect of an After-Meal Candy on Restaurant Tipping

Bruce Rind

Affiliation

uses *subheadings* placed at the left margin (flush left), underlined, and in uppercase and lowercase. If she wished to use a further level of subheadings, they would be indented, underlined, and followed by a period, with the body of the text immediately following the heading, for example:

<u>Seven Kinds of Intelligence</u>

    <u>Logical-Mathematical</u>. One type of intelligence that has been thoroughly examined is generally referred to . . .

Underlining

As the previous example shows, *underlining* can be used to distinguish levels of headings. Conventional usage also calls for the titles of books mentioned in the body of the text to be underlined ("In <u>Pygmalion in the Classroom,</u> Rosenthal and Jacobson . . ."). Underlining is also used in several other ways:

- Letters used as statistical symbols are underlined: $\underline{F}$, $\underline{N}$, $\underline{n}$, $\underline{P}$, $\underline{p}$, $\underline{t}$, $\underline{Z}$, and so forth. The purpose of this underlining is to indicate that the symbols should be italicized when they are printed. Although it is just as easy for you to italicize as underline, many instructors prefer the underlining (and this is what is shown in the sample papers). However, if your instructor approves, then it is also acceptable to simply italicize the symbols (for example, *F, N, n, P, p, t, Z*).
- Note that some symbols are in lowercase, and this can be very important. For example, an underlined capital $\underline{N}$ indicates the total number of sampling units, but a lowercase $\underline{n}$ indicates the number of units in a subsample of N. Many instructors also prefer that you avoid capitalizing t if you mean Student's t test, because a capital letter implies a quite different statistic.
- However, Greek letters used as statistical symbols are not underlined, for example, the symbol for chi-square (χ^2), the symbol telling us to sum a set of scores (Σ), the symbol for the standard deviation of a set of scores (σ), and the symbol for the variance of a set of scores (σ^2).
- In reference lists, volume numbers of journal articles and titles of books and journals are underlined.
- Words that you wish to emphasize are underlined, but underlining should be done sparingly ("Effective teaching, the authors assert, will come only from the teachers' firm belief that their pupils <u>can</u> perform . . .").
- Words used as terms are also underlined ("the term <u>knowing</u> . . ." or ". . . is called <u>knowing</u> . . ."). For example, Anne writes, "People use the term <u>intelligence</u> . . ." and "Some individuals are called <u>book smart,</u> a term meaning . . .").

APA also does not return technical manuscripts in which statistical symbols in equations are italicized rather than underlined. So if you are using a program (such as *MathType*) in which it may be easier to italicize than to underline statistical symbols in equations, that is OK. An example appears in the final paragraph of Bruce's Results section.

Citations in Text

There are several simple conventions for citing an author's work in the narrative of a paper. The purpose of a citation is to make it easy for the reader to identify the source of a quotation or idea and then to locate the particular reference in the list at the end of the paper. The author-date method is the format recommended by the APA publication manual. The surname of the author and the year of publication are inserted in the narrative text at the appropriate point.

Here are two general rules, and some exceptions:

- ◆ Do not list any publication in your reference list that you do not cite. The exception to this rule would be if you were developing an extensive bibliography of references, but you would not usually do that for an essay paper or research report.
- ◆ Do not cite any reference without placing it in the reference list. The exception to this rule would be citing a personal communication or an entire Web site (as illustrated below).

If you want to cite a source that you did not read, make it clear that you are borrowing someone else's citation. But do this only if the original source is unavailable to you; otherwise examine and cite the original source yourself.

Citation of Unread Source

> In Virgil's epic poem, <u>The Aeneid,</u> as cited by Allport and Postman (1947), the following characterization of rumor appears: . . .

In general, there are two categories of citations in student research reports and essays (you will find many examples of each in the three sample papers). One category consists of citations that appear as part of the narrative; the other category consists of citations inserted in alphabetical order (and then by year if the same author is cited twice) entirely in parentheses within the narrative. Notice in the first example below that the word *and* is spelled out in a narrative citation, whereas in the second example an ampersand (&) is used in a parenthetical citation:

Citation Appearing as Part of Narrative

> Baldwin, Doyle, Kern, and Stella (1991) asked a sample of child-care providers to describe incidents in which . . .

Citation Entirely in Parentheses

> Institutional review boards may harbor quite different biases regarding the ethical risks of the studies they are asked to evaluate (e.g., Ceci,

Peters, & Plotkin, 1985; Hamsher & Reznikoff, 1967; Kallgren & Kenrick, 1990; Schlenker & Forsyth, 1977).

These examples also illustrate the convention of author-date citations that dictates the listing of the surnames of up to five authors the first time the citation is given. In subsequent citations, if there are more than two authors, you mention the surname of only the first author followed by *et al.* (neither underlined nor in italics, however) and the date, for example:

Subsequent Citation as Part of Narrative

Ceci et al. (1985) found that one research proposal, approved without changes in one institution, was amended at another institution in the same city.

Subsequent Citation Entirely in Parentheses

One research proposal, approved without changes in one institution, was amended at another institution in the same city (Ceci et al., 1985).

To cite an E-mail note or a written communication (for example, a letter), you would cite it in the narrative as a personal communication; you would not list it again in your References section:

Personal Communication (such as E-mail Note) as Part of Narrative

An alternative approach, noted by T. E. Schoenfelder (personal communication, August 12, 1999), would explain investment decisions within the framework of behavioral decision theory.

Personal Communication (such as E-mail Note) in Parentheses

An alternative approach would explain investment decisions within the framework of behavioral decision theory (T. E. Schoenfelder, personal communication, August 12, 1999).

When citing E-mail correspondence, you must be certain that you are citing the source accurately, because it is possible for someone to send an E-mail note disguised as someone else.

The APA also recommends a specific citation format for citing a Web site (not a specific document obtained from a Web site); you would give the address of the site, but you would not include it in your References section:

Web Site Citation

If you have any further questions about the <u>Publication Manual of the American Psychological Association</u> (4th ed.), check out the APA Publication Manual Frequently Asked Questions Web site (http://www.apa.org/journals/faq.html).

To cite a specific document from a Web site, use a format similar to that for printed material (as shown above).

Here are some other specific rules that cover most of the cases that students encounter:

- If you are citing a series of works, the proper sequence is by alphabetical order of the surname of the first author and then by chronological order (Aditya, 1998, 2000; Brecher, 1999; DiClemente, 2000; DiFonzo & Bordia, 1993; Freeman, 1999; Gergen & Shotter, 1985, 1988; Stern, in press; Strohmetz, 1997; Trimble, in press; Wells & Lafleur, 1997).
- Two or more works published by the same author in the same year are designated as *a, b, c,* and so on (Hantula, 2000a, 2000b, 2000c). In the References section, the alphabetical order of the works' titles determines the sequence when there is more than one work by the author in the same year.
- Work accepted for publication but not yet printed is designated "in press" (Hesson, in press); in a list of citations, the rule is to place this work last: (Hesson, 1993, 1996, in press).

What should you do if you run into a problem that these rules do not address? You might check out the APA Web site noted above. However, even the APA seems quite flexible and does not return manuscripts simply because the format of one unusual citation deviates from the norm. Once the manuscript is accepted for publication, corrections are made during the copy-editing process. Thus, keep one general idea in mind as you go beyond these specific guidelines: *If you run into a problem, use common sense.* Ask yourself whether you could identify the reference based on the citation you have provided. In other words, put yourself in your reader's shoes.

Tables and Figures

Tables and figures may be used to augment the presentation of the results. Often, when students include tables in their research reports, the instructor finds that they are merely presenting their raw data in a neat format. Save your raw data for the appendix of your report (if your raw data are required), as shown in Bruce's report. Keep in mind that statistical tables in research reports should contain *summaries* of the raw data rather than the actual data (see, for example, Bruce's and Peter's tables) and other results.

The APA publication manual requires that tables and figures be put on separate pages at the end of the paper, numbered in the order in which they are first mentioned in the paper. Notice that the title of each table in Bruce's and Peter's papers is shown above the table. If these were figures, then the title (called the *caption*) would be shown below the figure. Table titles, in uppercase and lowercase letters, are flush left and underlined; figure captions are not underlined, begin with a capital letter, and end with a period. So if Peter had used a figure instead of a table, the figure caption might look like this:

Figure 1. Percentage of illustrations as a function of gender and work.

Each column of a table is expected to have a heading, including the left-most column (called the *stub column,* it usually lists the major independent variables). These column headings identify the items below them, and some tables use a hierarchy of headings (also known as *decked heads*) to avoid re-peating words. When the top heading in the hierarchy spans the body of the table, it is called a *table spanner.* Just remember to keep your table headings clear, concise, and informative, so the reader can easily understand what is in the table.

If you are confused about the difference between a table and a figure, think of figures as graphics that are photographed or imported from artwork (for example, bar charts and frequency polygons). The basic rule is to use fig-ures that add to the text; do not simply repeat what you can say very clearly in words in the text. Because figures sometimes introduce distortions that de-tract from a clear, concise summary of the data, most researchers prefer to use tables. If you must use a figure, be sure not to overcomplicate it; ask a friend if he or she understands it. The art of graphic design has also been studied by psychologists; if you would like to learn more on this subject, start with S. M. Kosslyn's *Elements of Graph Design* (W. H. Freeman, 1994).

However you choose to display your findings in the research report, the title or caption must be clearly and precisely stated. If you need to add some clarifying or explanatory note to your table, it is customary to place this in-formation below the table, for example:

Note. The possible range of scores was from 1 (strong disagreement) to 5 (strong agreement), with 3 indicating "no opinion."

If you want to make specific notes, the convention is to use superscript lowercase letters ([a] [b] [c]) or asterisks (* ** ***). The following cases illustrate this usage:

Superscript Notation

[a]$\underline{n} = 50$ [b]$\underline{n} = 62$

Asterisk Notation

*$\underline{p} < .05$ **$\underline{p} < .01$ ***$\underline{p} < .0005$

The following guidelines will prove helpful if you are preparing a figure:

◆ The figure should be neat, clearly presented, and precisely labeled to augment your discussion.
◆ The figure should be large enough to read easily.
◆ The units should progress from small to large.

- The data should be precisely plotted. If you are drawing the figure by hand, use graph paper to help you keep the rows and columns evenly spaced.
- When graphing the relationship between an independent and a dependent variable (or between a predictor variable and a criterion or outcome variable), it is customary to put the independent (or predictor) variable on the horizontal axis (called the x-axis, or the abscissa) and the dependent (or criterion) variable on the vertical axis (the y-axis, or ordinate).

List of References

The list of references starts on a new page, with the title "References" centered on the top of the page. The references are arranged alphabetically by the surname of the author(s) and then by the date of publication. The standard style recommended in the APA manual is to:

- Invert all authors' names (that is, last name, first initial, middle initial).
- List authors' names in the exact order in which they appear on the title page of the publication.
- Use commas to separate authors and an ampersand (&) before the last author.
- Give the year the work was copyrighted (the year and month for magazine articles and the year, month, and day for newspaper articles).
- For titles of books, chapters in books, and journal articles, capitalize only the first word of the title and of the subtitle (if any) as well as any proper names.
- Give the issue number of the journal if the article cited is paginated by issue.
- Underline the volume number of a journal article and the title of a book or a journal.
- Give the city and state of a book's publisher, using the postal abbreviations listed in Exhibit 17.
- However, major cities in the United States (such as Baltimore, Boston, Chicago, Los Angeles, New York, Philadelphia, and San Francisco) can be listed without a state abbreviation.
- If you are listing a foreign city other than Amsterdam, Jerusalem, London, Milan, Moscow, Paris, Rome, Stockholm, Tokyo, or Vienna, then list the country as well.

Using these pointers, the examples in the three sample papers, and the following examples as general guidelines, you should encounter few problems. If you do run into one, however, the rule of thumb is to be clear, consistent, and complete in listing your source material:

EXHIBIT 17   Postal abbreviations for states and territories

Location	Abbreviation	Location	Abbreviation
Alabama	AL	Montana	MT
Alaska	AK	Nebraska	NE
Arizona	AZ	Nevada	NV
Arkansas	AR	New Hampshire	NH
California	CA	New Jersey	NJ
Colorado	CO	New Mexico	NM
Connecticut	CT	New York	NY
Delaware	DE	North Carolina	NC
District of Columbia	DC	North Dakota	ND
Florida	FL	Ohio	OH
Georgia	GA	Oklahoma	OK
Guam	GU	Oregon	OR
Hawaii	HI	Pennsylvania	PA
Idaho	ID	Puerto Rico	PR
Illinois	IL	Rhode Island	RI
Indiana	IN	South Carolina	SC
Iowa	IA	South Dakota	SD
Kansas	KS	Tennessee	TN
Kentucky	KY	Texas	TX
Louisiana	LA	Utah	UT
Maine	ME	Vermont	VT
Maryland	MD	Virginia	VA
Massachusetts	MA	Virgin Islands	VI
Michigan	MI	Washington	WA
Minnesota	MN	West Virginia	WV
Mississippi	MS	Wisconsin	WI
Missouri	MO	Wyoming	WY

Authored Book

Single Author

Lana, R. E. (1991). <u>Assumptions of social psychology: A reexamination.</u> Hillsdale, NJ: Erlbaum.

Two Authors

Levin, J., & Arluke, A. (1987). <u>Gossip: The inside scoop.</u> New York: Plenum Press.

More than two Authors

Webb, E. J., Campbell, D. T., Schwartz, R. D., & Sechrest, L. (1966). Unobtrusive measures: Nonreactive research in the social sciences. Chicago: Rand McNally.

Institutional Author and Publisher

American Psychological Association. (1994). Publication manual of the American Psychological Association (4th ed.). Washington, DC: Author.

Work in Press

Edited Volume

Kowalski, R. M. (Ed.). (in press). The underbelly of social interaction: Aversive interpersonal behaviors. Washington, DC: American Psychological Association.

Journal Article

Bordia, P., DiFonzo, N., & Schulz, C. A. (in press). Source characteristics in denying rumors of organizational closure: Honesty is the best policy. Journal of Applied Social Psychology.

Chapter in Edited Book

Aditya, R. N., & House, R. J. (in press). Interpersonal acumen and leadership across cultures: Pointers from the GLOBE study. In R. E. Riggio & S. E. Murphy (Eds.), Multiple intelligences and leadership. Mahwah, NJ: Erlbaum.

Authored Book

Doyle, W. (in press). Inside the oval office: The White House from FDR to Clinton. New York: Kodansha.

Edited Published Work

Single Editor

Morawski, J. G. (Ed.). (1988). The rise of experimentation in American psychology. New Haven, CT: Yale University Press.

Two Editors

Goodman, R. F., & Ben-Ze'ev, A. (Eds.). (1994). Good gossip. Lawrence: University Press of Kansas.

Work Republished at a Later Date

Book of Collected Work

Demosthenes. (1852). The Olynthiac and other public orations of Demosthenes. London: Henry G. Bohn. (Original work written 349 B.C.)

Single Volume in Multivolume Series of Collected Work

Lessing, G. E. (1779/1971). <u>Gotthold Ephraim Lessing: Werke</u> (Vol. 2). München, Germany: Carl Hanser Verlag.

Chapter in an Anthology

Pope, A. (1733/1903). Moral essays: Epistle I. To Sir Richard Temple, Lord Cobham, of the knowledge and character of men. In H. W. Boynton (Ed.), <u>The complete poetical works of Pope</u> (pp. 157-160). Boston: Houghton Mifflin.

Article or Chapter

Article in Journal Paginated by Volume (Single Author)

Scott-Jones, D. (1994). Ethical issues in reporting and referring in research with low-income minority children. <u>Ethics and Behavior, 42,</u> 97-108.

Article in Journal Paginated by Volume (Multiple Authors)

Imber, S. D., Glanz, L. M., Elkin, I., Sotsky, S. M., Boyer, J. L., & Leber, W. R. (1986). Ethical issues in psychotherapy research: Problems in a collaborative clinical trials study. <u>American Psychologist, 41,</u> 137-146.

Chapter in Edited Book

Holton, G. (1978). From the endless frontier to the ideology of limits. In G. Holton & R. S. Morison (Eds.), <u>Limits of scientific inquiry</u> (pp. 227-241). New York: Norton.

Article in Encyclopedia Paginated by Volume

Stanley, J. C. (1971). Design of controlled experiments in education. In L. C. Deighton (Ed.), <u>The encyclopedia of education</u> (Vol. 3, pp. 474-483). New York: Macmillan and Free Press.

Article in Newsletter Paginated by Issue

Goldstein, J. H. (1978). In vivo veritas: Has humor research looked at humor? <u>Humor Research Newsletter, 3</u>(1), 3-4.

Article in Journal Paginated by Issue

Valdiserri, R. O., Tama, G. M., & Ho, M. (1988). The role of community advisory committees in clinical trials of anti-HIV agents. <u>IRB: A Review of Human Subjects Research, 10</u>(4), 5-7.

Non-English Publication

Book

Gniech, G. (1976). <u>Störeffekte in psychologischen Experimenten</u> [Artifacts in psychological experiments]. Stuttgart, Germany: Verlag W. Kohlhammer.

Journal Article

Foa, U. G. (1966). Le nombre huit dans la socialization de l'enfant [The number eight in the socialization of the infant]. <u>Bulletin du Centre d'Études et Recherches Psychologigues, 15,</u> 39-47.

Chapter in Multivolume Edited Series

Different Author and Editor

Kipnis, D. (1984). The use of power in organizations and interpersonal settings. In S. Oskamp (Ed.), <u>Applied social psychology</u> (Vol. 5, pp. 171-210). Newbury Park, CA: Sage.

Same Author and Editor

Koch, S. (1959). General introduction to the series. In S. Koch (Ed.), <u>Psychology: A study of a science</u> (Vol. 1, pp. 1-18). New York: McGraw-Hill.

Mass Media Article

Magazine Article

Rowan, R. (1979, August 13). Where did <u>that</u> rumor come from? <u>Fortune,</u> pp. 130-137.

Newspaper Article (Author Listed)

Grady, D. (1999, October 11). Too much of a good thing? Doctor challenges drug manual. <u>The New York Times,</u> Section F, pp. 1, 2.

Newspaper Article (No Author)

A toast to Newton and a long-lived "Principia." (1999, October 11). <u>The New York Times,</u> Section F, p. 4.

Dictionary or Encyclopedia

Dictionary (No Author)

<u>Random House dictionary of the English language.</u> (1966). New York: Random House.

Encyclopedia

Deighton, L. C. (Ed.). (1971). <u>The encyclopedia of education</u> (Vols. 1-10). New York: Macmillan and Free Press.

Doctoral Dissertation or Master's Thesis

Doctoral Dissertation Abstract

Esposito, J. (1987). Subjective factors and rumor transmission: A field investigation of the influence of anxiety, importance, and belief on rumormongering (Doctoral dissertation, Temple University, 1986). Dissertation Abstracts International, 48, 596B.

Unpublished Doctoral Dissertation

Smith, C. (1969). Selecting a source of local television news in the Salt Lake City SMSA: A multivariate analysis of cognitive and affective factors for 384 randomly-selected news viewers. Unpublished doctoral dissertation, Temple University School of Communication, Philadelphia.

Master's Thesis

Aditya, R. N. (1996). The not-so-good subject: Extent and correlates of pseudovolunteering in research. Unpublished master's thesis, Temple University, Philadelphia.

Unpublished Material

Technical Report

Kipnis, D., & Kidder, L. H. (1977). Practice performance and sex: Sex role appropriateness, success and failure as determinants of men's and women's task learning capabilities (Report No. 1). Philadelphia: University City Science Center.

Manuscript

Burnham, J. R. (1966). Experimenter bias and lesion labeling. Unpublished manuscript, Purdue University, West Lafayette, IN.

Paper Presented at a Meeting (Single Author)

Wells, C. V. (1997). Intraorganizational trust and influence in the mirror of change and diversity. Paper presented at the annual meeting of the Eastern Psychological Association, Washington, DC.

Paper Presented at a Meeting (Multiple Authors)

Rajala, A. K., DeNicolis, J. L., Brecher, E. G., & Hantula, D. A (1995). Investing in occupational safety: A utility analysis perspective. Paper presented at the annual meeting of the Eastern Academy of Management, Ithaca, NY.

Poster Presented at a Meeting

Freeman, M. A. (1995). Demographic correlates of individualism and collectivism: A study of social values in Sri Lanka. Poster presented at the annual meeting of the American Psychological Society, New York.

World Wide Web References

Abstract from PsycINFO Database

Morgeson, F. P., Seligman, M. E., Sternberg, R. J., Taylor, S. E., & Manning, C. M. (1999). Lessons learned from a life in psychological science: Implications for young scientists [Abstract]. <u>American Psycholo-gist, 54,</u> 106-116. Retrieved October 14, 1999, from the World Wide Web: http://www.spider.apa.org.html.

Article from PsycINFO Databasee

Egeth, H. E. (1993). What do we <u>not</u> know about eyewitness identi-fication? <u>American Psychologist, 48,</u> 577-580. Retrieved October 14, 1999, from the World Wide Web: http://www.spider.apa.org.html.

Information from Web Site

American Psychological Association. (1999). Scholarships, grants and funding opportunities. Retrieved October 14, 1999, from the World Wide Web: http://www.apa.org/students/grants.html.

Proofing and Correcting

We now come to the final steps before you submit your paper: proofing and correcting. Read the finished paper more than once. Ask yourself the follow-ing questions:

- ◆ Are there omissions?
- ◆ Are there misspellings?
- ◆ Are the numbers correct?
- ◆ Are the hyphenations correct?
- ◆ Do all the references cited in the body of the paper also appear in the References section?

The first time you read your final draft, the appeal of the neat, clean copy may lead you to overlook errors. Put the paper aside for 24 hours, and then read it carefully again. After you have corrected any errors, give the paper a final look, checking to be sure all the pages are there and in order. If you ad-hered to the guidelines in this manual, you should have the sense of a job well done and should feel confident that the paper will receive the serious atten-tion that a clear, consistent, and attractive manuscript deserves.

Appendix A

SAMPLE ESSAY

The Multiplex Versus g-centric View of Intelligence:

With Particular Emphasis on Gardner's Theory

Anne A. Skleder

Term Paper

(Number and Name of Course)

Instructor: (Name)

(Date Submitted)

Abstract

Two views of intelligence are discussed, the g-centric and the multiplex positions. The g-centric view, which is the more traditional position, proceeds on the assumption that there is a common trait (g) in all existing measures of intelligence. The multiplex view, which is a recently developed position, is that there are many kinds of intelligence, and they do not necessarily have a common psychometric core. One leading multiplex theory is that formulated by Howard Gardner, which is discussed here. Two criticisms of multiplex theories of intelligence are examined, and the paper concludes with a broad overview of the direction of work in this area.

The Multiplex Versus g-centric View of Intelligence:

With Particular Emphasis on Gardner's Theory

People use the word <u>intelligence</u> and its various synonyms in many different ways to refer to distinct aptitudes. Some individuals are called <u>book smart,</u> a term meaning that they are strong in verbal or mathematical aptitudes. Others are referred to as <u>street smart,</u> a term implying that they are intellectually shrewd in the ways of the world. Still others are said to have "business savvy" or "political sense" or the ability to "read people like a book," phrases meaning that their skills involve interpersonal aptitude that may not be directly measured by standard tests of intelligence. This essay looks at intelligence from two different viewpoints. One approach is sometimes characterized as the <u>g-centric view,</u> which reflects the psychometric idea of a general trait at the core of intelligence (g). The second approach, which is more recent, is characterized here as the <u>multiplex view,</u> which reflects the assumption of multiple intelligences housed within the same culture but not necessarily in any single individual within that culture. I begin by elaborating on the distinction between these two approaches and then focus on one prominent example of the multiplex view, the work of Howard Gardner (1983, 1985). Two main criticisms of multiplex theories are examined, and the paper concludes with a broad overview of the direction of work in this area.

Two Views of Intelligence

The Traditional View

For much of the 20th century, psychological research on intelligence focused on the existence of a general overriding trait of intelligence, usually measured by various short-answer tests of mathematical and linguistic skills. Influenced by the theoretical and psychometric contributions of Charles Spearman (1927), who regarded intelligence as a general characteristic, researchers in the intelligence test movement have usually accepted as valid the g-centric (or g-centered) notion of intelligence. A number of psychometricians, such as Arthur Jensen (1969), have further argued that differences in g can be attributed largely to "heritability" (genetic factors) as opposed to environmental or cultural influences, a position that has been hotly contested in psychology and education.

Regarding the essential idea of a general characteristic of intelligence, child development researchers inspired by the theoretical and empirical work of Jean Piaget have also argued for the idea of general structures of the mind (Siegler & Richards, 1982). These structures, they assert, develop in a similar way in all children. In the biological area, some investigators have attempted to operationalize g by measuring the speed of neural transmission (Reed & Jensen, 1992) or using measures of hemispheric localization (Levy, 1974). In the 1990s, a controversial reanalysis of IQ test data by Herrnstein and Murray (1994), in a book entitled The Bell Curve, ignited a spirited debate (e.g., Andery & Serio, 1997; Andrews & Nelkin, 1996; Carroll, 1997; Cullen, Gendreau, Jarjoura, & Wright, 1997; Ellis, 1998; Samelson, 1997; Yee, 1997) about the presumed role of g in the lives of individuals and in the larger social order.

Although the traditional view of intelligence has been periodically challenged, many experts consider fundamental the idea that standard IQ tests provide magical numbers that allow us to distinguish "bright" people from the "not-so-bright" in terms of accrued knowledge or potential for learning. Thus, whether a psychologist means by intelligence (a) the ability to adapt to the environment, (b) the ability to deal with symbols or abstractions, or (c) the ability to learn, most apparently assume that a core ingredient in these aptitudes is the factor known as g (Gilbert, 1971).

One early criticism of this view was articulated by L. L. Thurstone (1938) and his coworkers. On the basis of various psychometric studies they conducted with large numbers of participants, Thurstone and Thurstone (1941) concluded that there are distinct aptitudes, which they called "primary mental abilities," and which include verbal comprehension, word fluency, numerical ability, and spatial relations. More recently, Sternberg and Berg (1986) reported that a panel of experts embraced diverse, and ostensibly divergent, factors in what they theoretically associated with intelligence. Controversy surrounds the meaning of intelligence as well as its relation to real-world skills, but a task force of the American Psychological Association (APA) was nevertheless able to agree on a list of "knowns" about intelligence (Neisser et al., 1996).

The Multiplex View

Interestingly, Robert Sternberg (1990), 1 of 11 coauthors of that APA report, argued elsewhere that the nature of the information processing measured by standard IQ tests may be quite different from that involved in certain complex reasoning in everyday life. By way of illustration, Ceci and Liker (1986) reported that skill in handicapping racehorses could not be predicted from the handicapper's performance on the Wechsler Adult Intelligence Scale. Sternberg, Wagner, Williams, and Horvath (1995) concluded that "even the most charitable estimates of the relation between intelligence test scores and real-world criteria such as job performance indicate that approximately three fourths of the variance in real-world performance is not accounted for by intelligence test performance" (p. 912).

Sternberg's (1985, 1988, 1990) triarchic theory of intelligence is emblematic of the view characterized here as multiplex, because it encompasses the assumption of multiple intelligences, including some that operate beyond the verbal or mathematical realm (see also Ceci, 1990; Gardner, 1983). In the remainder of this essay, I will focus on another prominent example of the multiplex view, the theory of multiple intelligences that was advanced by Gardner (1983, 1993b). Gardner has also argued against the single general characteristic assumption and instead uses the term intelligences to embrace multiple intellectual aptitudes.

Gardner's Theory of Multiple Intelligences

Gardner's Notion of Intelligence

Gardner (1983) described intelligence as encompassing "the ability to solve problems, or to create products that are valued within one or more cultural settings" (p. x). In spite of this rather broad definition, he went on to argue that not every real-life skill should be regarded as belonging under the label of intelligence. Rather, he maintained that any talent deemed "intellectual" must fit the following eight criteria:

1. The potential must exist to isolate the intelligence by brain damage.

2. Exceptional populations, such as savants, whose members exhibit outstanding but uneven abilities, must provide evidence for the distinctive existence of the particular entity.

3. There must be identifiable core operations, that is, basic information-processing operations that are unique to the particular abilities.

4. There must be a distinctive developmental history, that is, stages through which individuals pass, with individual differences in the ultimate levels of expertise achieved.

Intelligence   7

5. There should be locatable antecedents (more primitive, less integrated versions) of the intelligence in other species.

6. The intelligence must be open to experimental study, so that predictions of the construct can be subjected to empirical tests.

7. Although no single standardized test can measure the entirety of abilities that are deemed intellectual, standardized tests should provide clues about the intelligence and should predict the performance of some tasks and not others.

8. It must be possible to capture the information content in the intelligence through a symbol system, for example, language or choreographed movements.

Seven Kinds of Intelligence

Using these requirements as a base, Gardner argued the importance of studying people within the "normal" range of intelligence, but also studying those who are gifted or expert in various domains valued by different cultures (see Gardner, 1993a). Gardner further emphasized the importance of studying individuals who have suffered selective brain injuries. Using his eight criteria and the research results from four major disciplines (psychology, sociology, anthropology, and biology), he proposed the existence of seven intelligences: (a) logical-mathematical, (b) linguistic, (c) spatial, (d) bodily-kinesthetic, (e) musical, (f) intrapersonal, and (g) interpersonal.

According to Gardner, traditional intelligence, which is language-based and easy to quantify by conventional measures, encompasses logical-mathematical intelligence and linguistic intelligence. People who are high in logical-mathematical intelligence are identified as skilled in reasoning and computation. People with keen linguistic skills are good with words and language. Gardner maintained, however, that these two kinds of intelligence represent only part of the picture. Thus, he theorized five additional kinds of intelligence.

Spatial intelligence is demonstrated by those who are able to navigate the spatial world with ease. Bodily-kinesthetic intelligence is the domain of dancers, athletes, neurosurgeons, and others skilled in carrying and moving their bodies. A person who is musically intelligent is talented in discerning themes in music and is sensitive to qualities of melody (e.g., pitch, rhythm, and timbre). The last two intelligences are part of what Gardner termed the "personal intelligences," that is, the talent to detect various shades of meaning in the emotions, intentions, and behavior of oneself (intrapersonal intelligence) and others (interpersonal intelligence). Those who are high in intrapersonal intelligence are adept at self-understanding; those who are high in interpersonal intelligence are said to be "people persons" who have a fix on the social landscape.

Independence of Abilities

Crucial to Gardner's formulation of multiple intelligences is the idea that the various "talents" are not necessarily linked. Someone may perform very poorly in one area (e.g., logical-mathematical) and yet perform well in others (e.g., spatial). This discrepancy calls to mind the stereotype of the brilliant but absent-minded chemistry professor, who cannot find the car in the parking lot but can describe in intricate detail the inner workings of molecules, and perhaps of automobiles. Different intelligences can exist and can presumably be measured quite independently of one another, according to Gardner's theory. Unfortunately, Gardner (1991b, 1993b) argued, because logical-mathematical and linguistic intelligences are valued so highly in American education, tests meant to measure a variety of intelligences still rely heavily on mathematical and verbal skills.

In other words, conventional tests of intelligence measure the same intelligences in slightly different, and perhaps trivial, ways. Therefore, it is not surprising that factor-analytic research (e.g., Spearman, 1927) has often demonstrated a correlation among certain abilities (implying the g factor), so that individuals who score higher in verbal intelligence tend to score higher than average in reasoning ability. Knowing someone's linguistic intelligence, however, does not necessarily tell us very much about the person's skills with people or music, or in any other realm.

The independence of abilities is also suggested by the fact that while intelligence tests predict school grades reasonably well, they are far less useful in predicting routine successes outside the school setting. Barring low levels of traditional IQ, managerial skills, for example, may be related much more to the ability to manage oneself and the task completion of others, or to the ability to interpret the actions and intentions of others, than to the ability to score high on a standard IQ test or some surrogate measure of academic intelligence (Aditya, 1997; Sternberg, 1988). Sternberg (1988, p. 211) called these extracurricular skills "practical intelligence" (and distinguished them from academic intelligence), which in this case seems to be heavily dependent on what Gardner called the personal intelligences.

Two Main Criticisms of Multiplex Theories

Nontraditional Orientation

Most criticisms of multiplex theories appear to rest on the distinction between intelligence and abilities that have been traditionally characterized as

talent (Walters & Gardner, 1986). For example, Ericsson and Charness (1994)
argued that expert performance does not usually reflect innate abilities and
capacities but is mediated predominantly by physiological adaptations and
complex skills. Gardner's (1995) response was that the issue is not whether
children are born with innate abilities or capacities, but whether a child who has
begun to work in a domain finds a skill and ease in performance that encourage
him or her to persevere in the effort. That most people do not usually think of
performance skills as "intellectual" is a red herring in this debate, a reflection of
the fact that we are still burdened by the traditional idea of intelligence, according
to Gardner. Sternberg (1990) reminded us that an individual who has experienced
an injury that causes a loss of bodily-kinesthetic ability is not viewed as "mentally
retarded." I would add that a person who is very low in social skills, but who
scores in the range of normal on IQ tests, is regarded neither as "mentally
retarded" nor as "socially retarded."

In short, Gardner's argument is that all the forms of intelligence he proposed
may be given equal consideration with the logical-mathematical and linguistic forms
so highly valued in Western cultures (Walters & Gardner, 1986). As he put it,
"When one revisits the psychological variable that has been most intensively
studied, that of psychometric intelligence or g, one finds little evidence to suggest
that sheer practice, whether deliberate or not, produces large ultimate differences in
performance" (Gardner, 1995, p. 802). Perhaps it is merely because experts have
chosen to consider g and the "academic intelligences" more important than the
personal intelligences that the term socially retarded is not in common use.
However, interest in social proclivities may lead to increased attention to the

interplay of the personal intelligences and success (cf. Aditya & House, in press; Rosnow, Skleder, Jaeger, & Rind, 1994; Sternberg, 1997).

Structure and Amenability to Tests

A second criticism is that, given the amorphous nature of multiplex theories, there are unlimited possibilities of adding to the number of intelligences, beyond even the seven described by Gardner. Since the initial presentation of his theory, he has suggested the possibility of more than seven intelligences and considers the seven to be "working hypotheses" fully amenable to revision after further investigation (Walters & Gardner, 1986). Whether this second criticism is reasonable or not depends on one's willingness to regard intelligence as even more inclusive of human talents than it is now.

Also, it has been argued that the standard psychometric approach has the distinct advantage of being more amenable to testing and measurement than is the theory of multiple intelligences. Gardner, on the other hand, has contended that his seven intelligences are measurable but that conventional tests are inadequate for the job. He has proposed measurements that are more closely linked to what people do in their daily lives—inside and outside academic settings. For example, in applying his theory to education, Gardner (1991a, 1993b) reported assessing children's intelligences by studying their school compositions, choice of activities, performance in athletic events, and other aspects of their behavior and cognitive processes. While this approach is certainly more difficult and complex than the old approach, such measurements are essential from the standpoint of Gardner's theory.

Conclusions

The challenge still remains to develop innovative ways (however complex and nontraditional) to measure the different facets of intelligence (Gardner, Kornhaber, & Wake, 1996; Neisser et al., 1996; Sternberg, 1992). In particular, I have concentrated on one formulation of the multiplex approach, Gardner's theory of multiple intelligences. This theory encompasses traditional aspects but also attempts to move our conceptualization of intelligence beyond those boundaries. For example, when Gardner (1983) described a great dancer as "kinesthetically intelligent," he alluded to a skill that Spearman would not have accepted as belonging within the category of intelligence. That Gardner's model is so much broader than the traditional model of intelligence is viewed from some perspectives as a problem because the broader the theory, the more difficult it is to disconfirm. However, based on my literature search, I discerned a trend toward broad, interdisciplinary formulations and definitions of intelligence as whatever mental abilities are necessary to enable us to shape and adapt to our environmental (e.g., Sternberg, 1997). With this broader approach, many researchers are now including a focus on assessing and improving performance skills that in the past were either ignored or considered far less significant than academic intelligence (e.g., Gardner, 1991b; Gardner et al., 1996; Sternberg, Torff, & Grigorenko, 1998).

Intelligence   13

References

Aditya, R. N. (1997). Toward the further understanding of managerial success: An exploration of interpersonal acumen. Unpublished doctoral dissertation, Temple University, Philadelphia.

Aditya, R. N., & House, R. J. (in press). Interpersonal acumen and leadership across cultures: Pointers from the GLOBE study. In R. E. Riggio & S. E. Murphy (Eds.), Multiple intelligences and leadership. Mahwah, NJ: Erlbaum.

Andery, M. A., & Serio, T. M. (1997). The Bell Curve: What has radical behaviorism to say about it? Behavior and Social Issues, 7, 69-82.

Andrews, L. B., & Nelkin, D. (1996). The Bell Curve: A statement. Science, 271(5245), 13-14.

Carroll, J. B. (1997). Psychometrics, intelligence, and public perception. Intelligence, 24, 25-32.

Ceci, S. J. (1990). On intelligence...more or less: A bioecologial treatise on intellectual development. Englewood Cliffs, NJ: Prentice Hall.

Ceci, S. J., & Liker, J. (1986). Academic and nonacademic intelligence: An experimental separation. In R. J. Sternberg & R. Wagner (Eds.), Practical intelligence: Origins of competence in the everyday world (pp. 119-142). New York: Cambridge University Press.

Cullen, F. T., Gendreau, P., Jarjoura, G. R., & Wright, J. P. (1997). Crime and the bell curve: Lessons from intelligent criminology. Crime and Delinquency, 43, 387-411.

Intelligence   14

Ellis, L. (1998). The evolution of attitudes about social stratification: Why many people (including social scientists) are morally outraged by <u>The Bell Curve.</u> <u>Personality and Individual Differences, 24,</u> 207-216.

Ericsson, K. A., & Charness, N. (1994). Expert performance: Its structure and acquisition. <u>American Psychologist, 49,</u> 725-747.

Gardner, H. (1983). <u>Frames of mind: The theory of multiple intelligences.</u> New York: Basic Books.

Gardner, H. (1985). <u>The mind's new science.</u> New York: Basic Books.

Gardner, H. (1991a). Assessment in context: The alternative to standardized testing. In B. R. Gifford & M. C. O'Connor (Eds.), <u>Changing assessments:</u> <u>Alternative views of aptitude, achievement and instruction</u> (pp. 77-119). Boston: Kluwer.

Gardner, H. (1991b). <u>The unschooled mind: How children think and how</u> <u>schools should teach.</u> New York: Basic Books.

Gardner, H. (1993a). <u>Creating minds: An anatomy of creativity seen through</u> <u>the lives of Freud, Einstein, Picasso, Stravinsky, Eliot, Graham, and Ghandi.</u> New York: Basic Books.

Gardner, H. (1993b). <u>Multiple intelligences: The theory in practice.</u> New York: Basic Books.

Gardner, H. (1995). Why would anyone become an expert? <u>American</u> <u>Psychologist, 50,</u> 802-803.

Gardner, H., Kornhaber, M. L., & Wake, W. K. (1996). <u>Intelligence: Multiple</u> <u>perspective.</u> Ft. Worth, TX: Harcourt Brace.

Intelligence   15

Gilbert, H. B. (1971). Intelligence tests. In L. C. Deighton (Ed.), The encyclopedia of education (Vol. 5, pp. 128-135). New York: Macmillan and Free Press.

Herrnstein, R. J., & Murray, C. (1994). The bell curve: Intelligence and class structure in American life. New York: Free Press.

Jensen, A. R. (1969). How much can we boost IQ and scholastic achievement? Harvard Educational Review, 39, 1-123.

Levy, J. (1974). Cerebral asymmetries as manifested in split-brain man. In M. Kinsbourne & W. L. Smith (Eds.), Hemispheric disconnection and cerebral function (pp. 165-183). Springfield, IL: Charles C Thomas.

Neisser, U., Boodoo, G., Bouchard, T. J., Jr., Boykin, A. W., Brody, N., Ceci, S. J., Halpern, D. F., Loehlin, J. C., Perloff, R., Sternberg, R. J., & Urbina, S. (1996). Intelligence: Knowns and unknowns. American Psychologist, 51, 77-101.

Reed, T. E., & Jensen, A. R. (1992). Conduction velocity in a brain nerve pathway of normal adult correlates with intelligence. Intelligence, 16, 259-272.

Rosnow, R. L., Skleder, A. A., Jaeger, M. E., & Rind, B. (1994). Intelligence and the epistemics of interpersonal acumen: Testing some implications of Gardner's theory. Intelligence, 19, 93-116.

Samelson, F. (1997). On the uses of history: The case of The Bell Curve. Journal of the History of the Behavioral Sciences, 33, 129-133.

Siegler, R. S., & Richards, D. D. (1982). The development of intelligence. In R. J. Sternberg (Ed.), Handbook of human intelligence (pp. 897-971). New York: Cambridge University Press.

Spearman, C. (1927). The abilities of man. New York: Macmillan.

Intelligence   16

Sternberg, R. J. (1985). Beyond IQ: A triarchic theory of human intelligence. New York: Cambridge University Press.

Sternberg, R. J. (1988). The triarchic mind: A new theory of human intelligence. New York: Viking.

Sternberg, R. J. (1990). Metaphors of mind: A new theory of human intelligence. New York: Cambridge University Press.

Sternberg, R. J. (1992). Ability tests, measurements, and markets. Journal of Educational Psychology, 84, 134-140.

Sternberg, R. J. (1997). The concept of intelligence and its role in lifelong learning and success. American Psychologist, 52, 1030-1037.

Sternberg, R. J., & Berg, C. A. (1986). Definitions of intelligence: A comparison of the 1921 and 1986 symposia. In R. J. Sternberg & D. K. Detterman (Eds.), What is intelligence? Contemporary viewpoints on its nature and definition (pp. 155-162). Norwood, NJ: Ablex.

Sternberg, R. J., Torff, B., & Grigorenko, E. L. (1998). Teaching triarchially improves school achievement. Journal of Educational Psychology, 90, 374-384.

Sternberg, R. J., Wagner, R. K., Williams, W. M., & Horvath, J. A. (1995). Testing common sense. American Psychologist, 50, 912-927.

Thurstone, L. L. (1938). Primary mental abilities. Chicago: University of Chicago Press.

Thurstone, L. L., & Thurstone, T. G. (1941). Factorial studies of intelligence. (Psychometric Society Psychometric Monographs No. 2). Chicago: University of Chicago Press.

Intelligence   17

Walters, J. M., & Gardner, H. (1986). The theory of multiple intelligences: Some issues and answers. In R. J. Sternberg & R. K. Wagner (Eds.), <u>Practical intelligence: Nature and origins of competence in the everyday world</u> (pp. 163-181). New York: Cambridge University Press.

Yee, A. H. (1997). Evading the controversy. <u>American Psychologist, 52,</u> 70-71.

Appendix B

SAMPLE EXPERIMENTAL RESEARCH REPORT

Tipping Behavior   1

Effect of an After-Meal Candy on Restaurant Tipping:

An Experimental Study in a Naturalistic Setting

Bruce Rind

Research Report

(Number and Name of Course)

Instructor: (Name)

(Date Submitted)

Abstract

Previous research has shown that waiters and waitresses (i.e., servers) can increase their tips by using a variety of techniques that generally involve creating an impression of friendliness. This study examined another technique that was expected to increase customers' favorable impressions of the server and, in turn, the size of the tip. The server in this study was provided with a basket of miniature chocolate candies, which she was instructed to bring with her when presenting the check in three experimental conditions. In one experimental condition, she offered each customer in the dining party one piece of candy of his or her choice. In a second experimental condition, she offered each person two pieces of candy. In a third experimental condition, she offered one candy and said, "Oh, have another piece" (the 1+1 condition). In the control condition, she presented the check as usual, without any candy offer. As hypothesized, offering candy increased tips, and offering more candies increased tips even more. Also as hypothesized, creating the impression that the gift reflected the server's generosity (the 1+1 condition) increased tips the most, a finding that was consistent with previous research on reciprocity.

Effect of an After-Meal Candy on Restaurant Tipping:

An Experimental Study in a Naturalistic Setting

More than 1 million people in the United States work as waiters or waitresses who serve in restaurants (Department of Commerce, 1990, p. 391). Although they are generally paid for their service by their employers, the major source of income for servers usually comes in the form of tips from customers (Lynn & Mynier, 1993; Schmidt, 1985). Because tips are so important to the livelihood of most servers, knowledge about factors that affect customers' tipping behavior is valuable. Recently, a growing number of studies have examined factors hypothesized to affect tipping. This research has shown that servers can increase their tipping percentages by a variety of techniques (Lynn, 1996).

Some of these techniques involve direct interpersonal action on the part of the server, such as touching or smiling at the customer. For example, Hornik (1992) had three waitresses at two restaurants either not touch their customers, touch them for half a second on the shoulder, or touch them twice on the palm of the hand for half a second each time. Tips increased from 12% to 14% to 17% in the three conditions, respectively. Tidd and Lockard (1978) had a waitress give customers sitting alone a large, open-mouth smile or a small, closed-mouth smile. Customers in the former condition tipped on average 48 cents compared to 20 cents in the latter condition. In a similar vein, Lynn and Mynier (1993) instructed servers either to squat to the eye level of their customers or stand erect during the initial visit to the table; the squatting increased tips. Garrity and Degelman (1990) reported that a server earned

higher tips when introducing herself by her first name during her initial visit (23%
average tip) than when she did not introduce herself (15% average tip).

Other effective techniques employed an indirect stimulus to encourage tipping.
Rind and Bordia (1996) had servers either draw or not draw a happy face on the
back of customers' checks before delivering them. The happy face increased tips for
the female server but did not increase tips for the male server (for whom this
practice may have been regarded as "gender-inappropriate" by customers). Rind
and Bordia (1995) also found that writing "thank you" on the back of checks
resulted in an increase in tips from 16% to 18%. Finally, McCall and Belmont
(1995) had servers present checks either on a tray with credit card emblems on it or
on a tray with no emblems and found that tipping percentages were higher in the
former condition.

These techniques, except for the last one, have in common that the servers are
doing something that may increase the customers' impressions of friendliness.
Another such technique was experimentally examined in the present study. When
presenting the check to the dining party, the server sometimes also presented a gift
of assorted candies. Three hypotheses were examined in this study. First, on the
assumption that the gift would be perceived by customers as a gesture of
friendliness, it was hypothesized that the presentation of the gift would have the
effect of increasing tips over a no-gift control condition. On the assumption that this
effect is cumulative (i.e., up to a certain point), the second hypothesis was that an
offer of more candies would increase tips even more. The third hypothesis was that
when customers were under the impression that the offer of a gift reflected the

server's rather than the restaurant's generosity, there would be an increase in tips. This third hypothesis was derived from research on reciprocity, which found that individuals felt especially obligated to return a favor to the person responsible for the favor (Regan, 1971).

Method

Participants

Eighty dining parties eating dinner at an upscale Italian-American restaurant located in central New Jersey served as participants. The total number of customers in the dining parties was 293, with a mean of 3.67 customers per dining party ($\underline{SD}$ = 1.97). The size of the dining parties ranged from 2 to 12.

Procedure

A female server, who also served as the experimental accomplice, was provided with a small wicker basket that was filled with Hershey Assorted Miniature chocolates. The candies were of four types: (a) dark chocolate bars, (b) milk chocolate bars, (c) rice and chocolate bars, and (d) peanut butter and chocolate bars. The server was also given a stack of 3-by-5-inch cards, each of which contained an instruction telling her to do one of four things when presenting the check. In the control condition, she was instructed to present the check as usual without any candy offer. In the three experimental conditions, she was instructed to bring along the basket of candy when presenting the check.

In one experimental condition, the server was instructed to offer each customer in the dining party one piece of candy of his or her choice (the "1-piece condition"). In a second experimental condition, she was instructed to offer each customer in the party two pieces of candy (the "2-piece condition"). In the third experimental condition, she was instructed to offer one candy and say, "Oh, have another piece," as if the offer were an afterthought (the "1+1 condition"); this treatment condition was intended to emphasize to customers the server's (as opposed to the restaurant's) generosity.

The cards were thoroughly shuffled to ensure that the order of the four types of instructions was random. When it was time to present the check, the server reached into her apron pocket and randomly chose a card. The server was instructed to thank the dining party upon their selection of candies, and then to leave the table immediately to avoid any nonessential interaction with the party. After the dining party had left the restaurant, the server recorded (on the same card used to determine the dining party's treatment condition) the amount of the tip left by the party, the amount of the bill before taxes, and the party size.

Results

The dependent measure was defined as the tip percentage, that is, the tip amount divided by the bill amount before taxes, which was then multiplied by 100. I did all the computations using a scientific calculator; the basic raw data (in percentages) and my calculations can be found at the end of this report. Table 1 reports the tip percentage (i.e., the arithmetic mean, M, of the percentages), the standard deviation (SD), and the sample size (n) in each condition. The statistical tests used were contrasts, which precisely addressed the three experimental hypotheses. In the method of contrast analysis, the prediction of interest is expressed in terms of integer values, called lambda (λ) weights, which must sum to zero.

First, to discover whether offering candy significantly increased tips, I contrasted the mean percentage of the no-mint group with the mean percentages of the three candy groups using a t test procedure described by Rosnow and Rosenthal (1996). The lambda weights I used were -3 for the control condition and +1, +1, +1 to represent each of the three experimental conditions. As shown in Table 1, the means of all three experimental conditions were higher than the mean of the control condition. The result of the contrast was $t(76) = 4.49$, one-tailed $p = .000013$.

The second hypothesis was that offering more candies would increase tips even more. To address this hypothesis, I compared the means of the 2-piece and 1+1-piece conditions (using λs of +1 and +1) with the 1-piece condition ($\lambda = -2$) and assigned $\lambda = 0$ to the no-candy condition. The result of this contrast was $t(76) = 4.70$, one-tailed $p = .000006$.

The third hypothesis, derived from reciprocity research, was that creating the impression that the gift reflected the server's generosity would increase the tip. I assigned lambda weights of +1 and -1 to the 1+1-piece and 2-piece conditions, respectively, and zero lambdas to the no-candy and 1-piece conditions. As indicated in Table 1, the average tip in the 1+1-piece condition was slightly larger than the average tip in the 2-piece condition. The contrast on these data yielded $t(76) = 2.06$, one-tailed $p = .022$.

The recent report of the American Psychological Association's Task Force on Statistical Inference stressed the importance of providing and interpreting effect sizes (e.g., d, g, or r) when publishing data in psychology journals (Wilkinson et al., 1999). The research in this paper is not currently being submitted for publication, but still I was hoping to identify the effect sizes. I could not use the standard calculations described in the textbook used in this course, because they were intended for two-group designs. In an advanced text by Rosenthal, Rosnow, and Rubin (2000), I found a detailed discussion of how to estimate $r_{effect\ size}$ from the contrast $\underline{t}$ test using the following formula:

$$r_{contrast} = \sqrt{\frac{t^2}{t^2 + df}},$$

where $\underline{df}$ denotes the degrees of freedom associated with the contrast $\underline{t}$ statistic. As Rosenthal et al. (2000) explained, $r_{contrast} = r_{effect\ size}$ in two-group designs, but $r_{contrast}$ may overestimate $r_{effect\ size}$ in designs with more than two groups. To find out whether $r_{contrast}$ is a good estimate of $r_{effect\ size}$ in designs with more than two groups, I correlated the lambda weights and group means (called the <u>alerting correlation</u>). When the alerting correlation approaches unity, it can be assumed that $r_{contrast}$ is a good estimate of $r_{effect\ size}$. Unfortunately, the alerting correlations in my study ranged from .30 to .69, and therefore I was unable to use the formula above to estimate the effect size correlation. Although other procedures for estimating $r_{effect\ size}$ were discussed by Rosenthal et al. (2000), they required more elaborate calculations than I was able to do in the limited time available to me. With the end of the semester fast approaching, I consulted with the instructor, who advised me not to attempt any further data analyses at this time.

Discussion

The results of this experiment suggest that adding a gift in the form of chocolate candies can increase servers' tip percentages; the more candy offered, the greater the tip. This finding is consistent with the assumption that offering a gift conveys a sense of friendliness to customers, who are inclined to be helpful by returning larger tips (cf. Lynn & Mynier, 1993). If creating a perception of friendliness was the mechanism, then this technique may be similar to many of the techniques reviewed by Lynn (1996). The last contrast reported here suggests the importance of reciprocity in increasing tips. That is, customers gave slightly larger tips when they were led to believe that the server was specifically responsible for the generosity of the gift.

Further research is needed to investigate the separate and interacting roles of reciprocity and perceptions of friendliness, and there is a need to verify the presumed role of "friendliness" that was implied by reciprocity research. Research is also needed to examine the generalizability of the current findings to male servers and other female servers, other types of restaurants (e.g., midscale), other regions of the country, and other types of gifts. I plan to continue the data analysis and to identify effect sizes using the procedures described in Rosenthal et al. (2000), and I then expect to submit my research as a poster for the next meeting of the Eastern Psychological Association.

References

Department of Commerce. (1990). <u>Statistical abstracts of the United States.</u> Washington, DC: Author.

Garrity, K., & Degelman, D. (1990). Effect of server introduction on restaurant tipping. <u>Journal of Applied Social Psychology, 20,</u> 168-172.

Hornik, J. (1992). Tactile stimulation and consumer response. <u>Journal of Consumer Research, 19,</u> 449-458.

Lynn, M. (1996). Seven ways to increase servers' tips. <u>Cornell Hotel and Restaurant Administration Quarterly, 37</u>(3), 24-29.

Lynn, M., & Mynier, K. (1993). Effect of server posture on restaurant tipping. <u>Journal of Applied Social Psychology, 23,</u> 678-685.

McCall, M., & Belmont, H. J. (1995). <u>Credit card insignia and tipping: Evidence for an associative link.</u> Unpublished manuscript, Ithaca College.

Regan, D. T. (1971). Effects of a favor and liking on compliance. <u>Journal of Experimental Social Psychology, 7,</u> 627-639.

Rind, B., & Bordia, P. (1995). Effect of server's "thank you" and personalization on restaurant tipping. <u>Journal of Applied Social Psychology, 25,</u> 745-751.

Rind, B., & Bordia, P. (1996). Effect of restaurant tipping of male and female servers drawing a happy, smiling face on the backs of customers' checks. <u>Journal of Applied Social Psychology, 26,</u> 218-225.

Rosenthal, R., Rosnow, R. L., & Rubin, D. B. (2000). Contrasts and effect sizes in behavioral research: A correlational approach. New York: Cambridge University Press.

Rosnow, R. L., & Rosenthal, R. (1996). Computing contrasts, effect sizes, and counternulls on other people's published data: General procedures for research consumers. Psychological Methods, 1, 331-340.

Schmidt, D. G. (1985). Tips: The mainstay of hotel workers' pay. Monthly Labor Review, 108, 50-61.

Tidd, K., & Lockard, J. (1978). Monetary significance of the affiliative smile: A case for reciprocal altruism. Bulletin of the Psychometric Society, 11, 344-346.

Wilkinson, L., & Task Force on Statistical Inference. (1999). Statistical methods in psychological journals: Guidelines and expectations. American Psychologist, 54, 594-605.

Table 1

Mean Tip Percentages, Standard Deviations, and Sample Sizes

in Four Treatment Conditions

	Treatment condition			
Results	No candy	1 piece	2 pieces	1+1 pieces
M	18.95	19.59	21.62	22.99
SD	1.50	1.75	2.51	2.49
n	20	20	20	20

Appendix

Raw Data and Calculation of Contrasts

no candy	1 piece	2 piece	1+1 piece
18.92	18.87	22.78	17.38
18.43	20.49	15.81	23.38
18.67	17.54	19.16	25.05
18.27	19.35	19.01	21.83
18.92	20.65	21.60	24.43
17.84	19.17	18.45	26.11
19.57	19.73	23.41	25.09
19.12	17.88	21.37	24.35
18.67	21.00	22.01	25.37
22.94	22.33	20.65	21.87
19.26	19.75	20.92	23.87
19.49	20.79	26.17	22.62
19.12	20.52	23.31	26.73
15.90	22.66	23.85	21.81
19.29	18.60	22.30	23.60
19.12	18.60	21.34	23.06
21.70	20.07	18.89	24.05
16.72	14.64	23.47	16.72
17.75	19.01	25.69	22.43
19.35	20.08	22.12	25.08

$$\text{Contrast} = \frac{\sum_{j=1}^{k} \overline{X}_j \lambda_j}{\sqrt{MSW \left(\sum_{j=1}^{k} \frac{\lambda_j^2}{n_j} \right)}}$$

$$\text{Contrast 1} = \frac{18.95(-3) + 19.59(1) + 21.62(1) + 22.99(1)}{\sqrt{4.45 \left(\frac{(-3)^2}{20} + \frac{1^2}{20} + \frac{1^2}{20} + \frac{1^2}{20} \right)}}$$

$$= \frac{7.3373}{1.634} = 4.49$$

$$\text{Contrast 2} = \frac{18.95(0) + 19.59(-2) + 21.62(1) + 22.99(1)}{\sqrt{4.45 \left(\frac{0^2}{20} + \frac{(-2)^2}{20} + \frac{1^2}{20} + \frac{1^2}{20} \right)}}$$

$$= \frac{5.4332}{1.155} = 4.70$$

$$\text{Contrast 3} = \frac{18.95(0) + 19.59(0) + 21.62(-1) + 22.99(1)}{\sqrt{4.45 \left(\frac{0^2}{20} + \frac{0^2}{20} + \frac{(-1)^2}{20} + \frac{1^2}{20} \right)}}$$

$$= \frac{1.3747}{.667} = 2.06$$

Appendix C

SAMPLE ARCHIVAL RESEARCH REPORT

Gender and Work   1

The Representation of Gender and Work in Children's Books:

An Archival Study Using Content Analysis

Peter B. Crabb

Research Report

(Number and Name of Course)

Instructor: (Name)

(Date Submitted)

Gender and Work   2

Abstract

This archival investigation used the method of content analysis to reveal how work and gender were portrayed in 300 pictures in 130 award-winning children's books published from 1937 to 1989. Two raters who independently coded the pictures were in substantial agreement about the type of work activity portrayed. Female characters were more often shown as working in the household, whereas male characters were more often shown as working outside the home. Using as my theoretical starting point the position developed by Bussey and Perry (1982), I propose that children's exposure to such representations might result in expectancies, interests, and competencies that direct girls and boys to model themselves after work roles defined by a traditional gender-based division of labor.

The Representation of Gender and Work in Children's Books:

An Archival Study Using Content Analysis

One of the main factors defining the division of labor in industrialized

societies is gender. Since the 18th century, women have typically been homemakers

and child-care givers and men have been wage earners working outside the home

(Parsons, 1955). In the United States and other countries, this division of labor has

changed, however. Since the late 1960s, the proportion of single and married

women working outside the home in the United States has increased dramatically

(Department of Labor, 1991). Despite this trend, there is evidence that children

continue to view work in and outside the home as gender-appropriate (Gettys &

Cann, 1981). This finding raises the possibility that children are being exposed to

stereotypical representations that link women to household work and men to work

outside the home.

One plausible source of such representations of gender and work may be

children's books. To examine how high-profile books for children portray work and

gender, I chose the method of content analysis. This method is traditionally used to

encode textual information but has also been used to encode qualitative data such as

verbal and action behavior (Boyatzis, 1998; Gottschalk, 1995; Roberts, 1997; Smith,

1992). It is possible to categorize qualitative data by having raters independently

tabulate the frequencies of occurrence of sampling units (also called recording units

and units of analysis) of theoretical interest (Elder, Pavalko, & Clipp, 1993;

Krippendorff, 1980; Stone, 1997). In the study reported in this paper, I had two

working hypotheses:

1. In comparison with male characters, a larger proportion of female characters would be shown doing household work in depictions of gender and work.

2. In comparison with female characters, a larger proportion of male characters would be shown doing production work.

Method

Unitizing Procedure

Krippendorff (1980, p. 57) used the term <u>unitizing</u> to refer to the process of defining and selecting the recording of sampling units in a content analysis. I defined the unit of analysis in this study as illustrations of gender and work found in award-winning children's books published in the United States from 1937 to 1989. Specifically, the sample of books chosen was identified as having received the Newbery or Caldecott awards (Association for Library Service to Children, 1990). Presumably, such books would have a high profile in libraries and bookstores and therefore were assumed to be representative of the reading material of American children. Only illustrations showing a character easily identified as male or female using a tool to perform some type of work were used in this analysis. I identified 1,613 such illustrations and, under the guidance of the instructor, pared them down by the method of proportionate sampling (Kish, 1965). This method uses random sampling to identify representative proportions of the specified categories of events (e.g., male characters and female characters using a tool to perform work). The original sample was thereby reduced to 300 relevant illustrations, of which 78 were of female characters and 222 were of male characters. This final sample included pictures from 130 of the 220 books and represented every publication year from 1937 to 1989.

Raters and Recording Procedure

    The procedure called <u>recording</u> refers to the coding of data, in which raters record the frequencies of occurrence of specific events or variables of theoretical interest (Krippendorff, 1980). The raters in this study were two female students enrolled in an introductory psychology course who volunteered to participate. They were instructed to use the coding sheet shown in Appendix A. For each book, the rater noted the author's (illustrator's) name, a designated code number, the year the book was published, and the book's place of publication, publisher, and total number of pages. In coding the illustrations, the raters noted (a) the page number of the illustration; (b) the tool shown in the picture; (c) the type of work represented (i.e., household, production, or other); (d) whether the person doing the work was a child, an adult, or unidentifiable as either; and also (e) whether that person was male, female, or unidentifiable by gender. The category <u>household work</u> was defined as "the use of tools in and around the home to prepare food, to clean, and to care for family members." The category production work was defined as "the use of tools outside the home for construction, agriculture, and transportation." The category <u>other work</u> was defined as "work that did not qualify as either household or production, including the use of tools for leisure activities and for protection from the elements."

Results

    The interrater reliability for coding the type of work was calculated by means of Cohen's kappa (κ), as described by Fleiss (1981); all computations are in Appendix B. The higher the value of kappa, the more the agreement indicated in the ratings of the two judges. These judges independently coded the type of work into three categories, with the resulting κ = .77. According to a general rule of thumb noted by Elder et al. (1993), this magnitude of kappa implied "substantial agreement" between the two judges.

Table 1 shows the results addressing the two hypotheses in this study. Consistent with the first hypothesis, there was a larger percentage of female characters than male characters portrayed as engaging in household work in the 55 illustrations of household work. According to a statistical procedure described by Fleiss (1981), the difference between the two percentages was statistically significant with a large magnitude of effect ($\underline{Z}$ = 5.68, one-tailed $\underline{p}$ = 6.7E-9, $\underline{r}_{effect\ size}$ = .77). Consistent with the second hypothesis, there was also a larger percentage of male characters than female characters engaged in production work outside the home in the 114 illustrations of production work ($\underline{Z}$ = 5.88, one-tailed $\underline{p}$ = 2.1E-9, $\underline{r}_{effect\ size}$ = .55).

Although I formulated no hypothesis, I was also interested in discovering whether the percentages of female and male characters doing work that was unrelated to household or production operations differed. A one-tailed $\underline{p}$ level is appropriate when a directional prediction is made, but a two-tailed $\underline{p}$ was required in this case because this was an ad hoc conjecture. For 131 illustrations showing other types of work, the effect was small ($\underline{r}_{effect\ size}$ = .11) and not statistically significant ($\underline{Z}$ = 1.31, two-tailed $\underline{p}$ = .19).

Discussion

This investigation addressed the question of whether the culturally supplied representations of gender and work in children's books reflected a stereotypical division of labor. As hypothesized, female characters tended to be shown working in the home, whereas male characters tended to be shown working outside the home. Work that is typically unrelated to either household operations or production activities was not portrayed as predominantly female or male. Thus this particular sample of children's books appears to reflect only traditional work roles for females and males.

The findings are theoretically important because of their modeling implications. The term modeling refers to the social phenomenon in which someone who observes someone else (a model) demonstrate certain behavior then copies the behavior. This phenomenon has been shown to be present in a range of situations involving adults who copy the behavior of others (Rosenthal, 1966). It seems plausible that children are susceptible to the effect of gender-linked modeling (Bussey & Perry, 1982). That is, children who observe the work behavior of characters in books may as a consequence become more interested in tools and skills modeled as appropriate for their own gender.

One limitation of this study, however, is that a small sample of award-winning books ending in 1989 was examined. It may be that other books, television, and other media more accurately reflect different trends in work roles that are current in our society. Another limitation is that I did not explore possible differences in the portrayal of work roles over time. Future research is needed to address these issues and to examine how pictorial representations affect children's expectations, attitudes, and behavior.

Gender and Work   8

References

Association for Library Service to Children. (1990). The Newbery and Caldecott awards. Chicago: American Library Association.

Boyatzis, R. E. (1998). Transforming qualitative information: Thematic analysis and code development. Thousand Oaks, CA: Sage.

Bussey, K., & Perry, D. G. (1982). Same-sex imitation: The avoidance of cross-sex models or the acceptance of same-sex models? Sex Roles, 8, 773-784.

Department of Labor. (1991). Working women: A chartbook (Bulletin 2385). Washington, DC: Bureau of Labor Statistics.

Elder, G. H., Jr., Pavalko, E. K., & Clipp, E. C. (1993). Working with archival data: Studying lives. Newbury Park, CA: Sage.

Fleiss, J. L. (1981). Statistical methods for rates and proportions. New York: Wiley.

Gettys, L. D., & Cann, A. (1981). Children's perceptions of occupational sex stereotypes. Sex Roles, 8, 301-308.

Gottschalk, L. A. (1995). Content analysis of verbal behavior: New findings and clinical applications. Hillsdale, NJ: Erlbaum.

Kish, L. (1965). Survey sampling. New York: Wiley.

Krippendorff, K. (1980). Content analysis: An introduction to methodology. Newbury Park, CA: Sage.

Parsons, T. (1955). The American family: Its relation to personality and social structure. In T. Parsons & R. F. Bales (Eds.), Family, socialization and interaction process (pp. 3-33). Glencoe, IL: Free Press.

Gender and Work   9

Roberts, C. W. (Ed.) (1997). Text analysis for the social sciences: Methods for drawing statistical inferences from texts and transcripts. Mahwah, NJ: Erlbaum.

Rosenthal, R. (1966). Experimenter effects in behavioral research. New York: Appleton-Century-Crofts.

Smith, C. P. (Ed.) (1992). Motivation and personality: Handbook of thematic content analysis. Cambridge: Cambridge University Press.

Table 1

Percentage of Illustrations as a Function of Gender and Work

Gender	Type of work		
	Household	Production	Other
Female	39.7	10.3	50.0
Male	10.8	47.8	41.4

Gender and Work   11

Appendix A

Coding Sheet Used by Raters

Gender and Work   12

| | | Author's, Illustrator's Name(s) | | | | | | Book # | | |

Pub. Date   Title

Place of Publication   Publisher

Pages

p.#	Tool Used	Work Type			Character						
		Hshold	Prdctn	Other	Age			Gender			
					Ch	Ad	?	F	M	?	

Gender and Work   13

Appendix B

Calculations on the Raw Data

Gender and Work   14

<u>Interjudge Agreement</u>

$\underline{N}$ = 300 illustrations

$\underline{n}$ = 2   judges

κ = 3   categories

$\underline{N_n}$ = 600

① $\sum n_j \text{ household}$ = 7+17+13+21+12+10+5+24+9+17+7 =   137

   $\sum n_j \text{ production}$ = 19+40+21+22+17+22+2+26+6+16+8 =   199

   $\sum n_j \text{ other}$ = 16+17+32+33+31+92+1+24+14+91+12 =   265

② $\sum n^2_{n_j} \text{ household}$ = 13+27+25+35+20+18+9+46+8+25+11 =   237

   $\sum n^2_{n_j} \text{ production}$ = 35+76+91+40+31+99+2+50+12+28+19 =   373

   $\sum n^2_{n_j} \text{ other}$ = 30+37+69+59+59+82+1+96+29+73+23 =   502

③ $P_{o \text{ household}}$ = $\frac{137}{600}$ = .2293

   $P_{o \text{ production}}$ = $\frac{199}{600}$ = .3317

   $P_{o \text{ other}}$ = $\frac{265}{600}$ = .4917

④ $\bar{P}_o = \frac{1}{N_n(n-1)}\left(\sum_{i=1}^{n}\sum_{j=1}^{2} n^2_{ij} - N_n\right)$

   $= \frac{1}{(300)(2)(2-1)}\left(502+237+373) - 300(2)\right)$

   $= \frac{1}{600}\left(1112-600\right)$

   $= .8533$

⑤ $\bar{P}_e = \sum_{j=1}^{k} P_j^2$

   $= (.4917)^2 + (.2283)^2 + (.3317)^2$

   $= .3572$

⑥ $Kappa = \dfrac{\bar{P}_o - \bar{P}_e}{1 - \bar{P}_e}$

   $= \dfrac{.8533 - .3572}{1 - .3572}$

   $= \boxed{+0.77}$

Hypothesis 1: $P_F > P_m$ (Household Work)

Total Sample: $\underline{N} = 300$, with $\underline{N}_F = 78$ and $\underline{N}_m = 222$

Illustrations of Household Work: $\underline{N} = 55$, with $\underline{n}_F = 31$, $\underline{n}_m = 24$

Note: $P =$ "big P", $p =$ "little p"

① $se_{P_F - P_m} = \sqrt{p(1-p)\left(\frac{1}{\underline{N}_F} + \frac{1}{\underline{N}_m}\right)}$, where $p = \dfrac{\underline{n}_F + \underline{n}_m}{\underline{N}_F + \underline{N}_m}$

$= \sqrt{.1833(.8167)\left(\frac{1}{78} + \frac{1}{222}\right)}$

$\qquad = \dfrac{31 + 24}{78 + 222}$

$= .0509$

$\qquad = .1833$

② $Z = \dfrac{P_F - P_m}{se_{P_F - P_m}}$, where $P_F = \dfrac{\underline{n}_F}{\underline{N}_F} = \dfrac{31}{78} = .3974$

$= \dfrac{.3974 - .1081}{.0509}$ and $P_m = \dfrac{\underline{n}_m}{\underline{N}_m} = \dfrac{24}{222} = .1081$

$= \boxed{5.68}$

③ Effect Size $\phi = \dfrac{Z}{\sqrt{N}}$

$= \dfrac{5.68}{\sqrt{55}}$

$= \boxed{+0.77}$

Gender and Work   16

$$\text{Hypothesis } 2 : P_F < P_m \quad (\text{Production Work})$$

Total Sample: $\underline{N} = 300$, with $\underline{N}_F = 78$ and $\underline{N}_m = 222$

Illustration of Production work: $\underline{N} = 114$, with $\underline{n}_F = 8$ and $\underline{n}_m = 106$

Note: $P = $ "big P", $p = $ "little p"

① $se_{P_m - P_F} = \sqrt{p(1-p)\left(\frac{1}{\underline{n}_F} + \frac{1}{\underline{N}_m}\right)}$, where

$$= \sqrt{.38(.62)\left(\frac{1}{78} + \frac{1}{222}\right)}$$

$$= .0638$$

$p = \dfrac{\underline{n}_F + \underline{n}_m}{\underline{N}_F + \underline{N}_m}$

$= \dfrac{8 + 106}{78 + 222}$

$= .38$

② $Z = \dfrac{P_m - P_F}{se_{P_m - P_F}}$, where $P_m = \dfrac{106}{222} = .478$

$P_F = \dfrac{8}{78} = .1026$

$= \dfrac{.478 - .1026}{.0638}$

$= \boxed{5.88}$

③ Effect Size $\phi = \dfrac{Z}{\sqrt{N}}$

$= \dfrac{5.88}{\sqrt{114}}$

$= \boxed{+0.55}$

Additional Test: $P_F = P_m$ (Other Work)

Total Sample : $N = 300$, $N_F = 78$, $N_m = 222$

Illustrations of Other Work : $N = 131$, $n_F = 39$, $n_m = 92$

Note: P = "big P", p = "little p"

① $se_{P_F - P_m} = \sqrt{p(1-p)\left(\frac{1}{N_F} + \frac{1}{N_m}\right)}$; where $p = \frac{n_F + n_m}{N_F + N_m}$

$= \sqrt{.4367(.5633)\left(\frac{1}{78} + \frac{1}{222}\right)}$ $= \frac{39 + 92}{78 + 222}$

$= .0656$ $= .4367$

② $z = \frac{P_F - P_m}{se_{P_F - P_m}}$, where $P_F = \frac{n_F}{N_F} = \frac{39}{78} = .50$

$= \frac{.50 - .4144}{.0656}$ $P_m = \frac{n_m}{N_m} = \frac{92}{222} = .4144$

$= \boxed{1.31}$

③ Effect Size $\phi = \frac{z}{\sqrt{N}}$

$= \frac{1.31}{\sqrt{131}}$

$= \frac{1.31}{11.45} = \boxed{+0.11}$

Index